Dicktales
or
"Thankyous and Sluggings"

Dicktales

or
"Thankyous and Sluggings"

The Irony
of Not
Being Able
to Invent
a New
Good Drink

by
Dick Bradsell

MIXELLANY

Illustration and photo credits: Alamy 20-21; Anistatia Miller 6-7, 61; dreamstime 1, 2-3, 4-5, 8, 34-35, 36-37, 38039, 40-41, 42-43, 44-45, 46-47, 48-49, 50; Eline Soo Yun Bosman 12, 62-63, 224-225; the estate of Dick Bradsell 5, 8, 14, 17, 18-19, 22-23, 25, 27, 28-29, 30-31, 32-33, 35, 36, 37, 38, 39, 40 41, 42, 43, 44, 45, 46, 47, 48, 49, 50, 51, 52, 53, 54, 56, 57, 64, 66, 67, 68, 69, 70,71, 72, 73, 74, 75, 76, 77, 78, 79, 80, 81, 82, 83, 84, 85, 86, 87, 88, 89, 90, 91, 92, 93, 94, 95, 96, 97, 98, 99, 100, 101, 102, 103, 104, 105, 106, 107, 108, 109, 110, 111, 112, 113, 114, 155, 116, 117, 118, 119, 120, 121, 122, 123, 124, 125, 126, 127, 128, 129, 130, 131, 132, 133, 134, 135, 136, 137, 138, 139, 140, 141, 142, 143, 144, 145, 146, 147, 148, 149, 150, 151, 152, 153, 154, 155, 156, 157, 158, 159, 184, 185, 187, 188, 189, 190, 191, 192, 193, 194, 195, 196, 197, 198 199, 200, 201, 203, 204-205, 207, 208, 209, 210, 211, 212, 213, 214, 215, 216, 217, 218, 219, 200, 221, 222, 223; Jared Brown 11, 162, 163, 164-165, 166-167, 168-169, 170-171, 172-173, 174-175, 176-177, 178-179, 180-181, 182-183, 226-227; Ned Conran 2; Olimax 206-213; Rita Keegan 130; shutterstock 6-7. 54-61, 64-75, 76-95, 96-109, 110-161, 162-183, 186-203

Edited by Anistatia Miller and Jared Brown
Text designed by Anistatia Miller
Cover design by Mateus Teixeira

Email: mixellanyltd@googlemail.com

First edition

British Library Cataloguing in Publication Data Available

ISBN: 978-1-907434-57-0 (hardcover);
ISBN: 978-1-907434-58-7 (tradepaper);
ISBN: 978-1-907434-63-1 (street edition);
ISBN: 978-1-907434-59-4 (ebook)

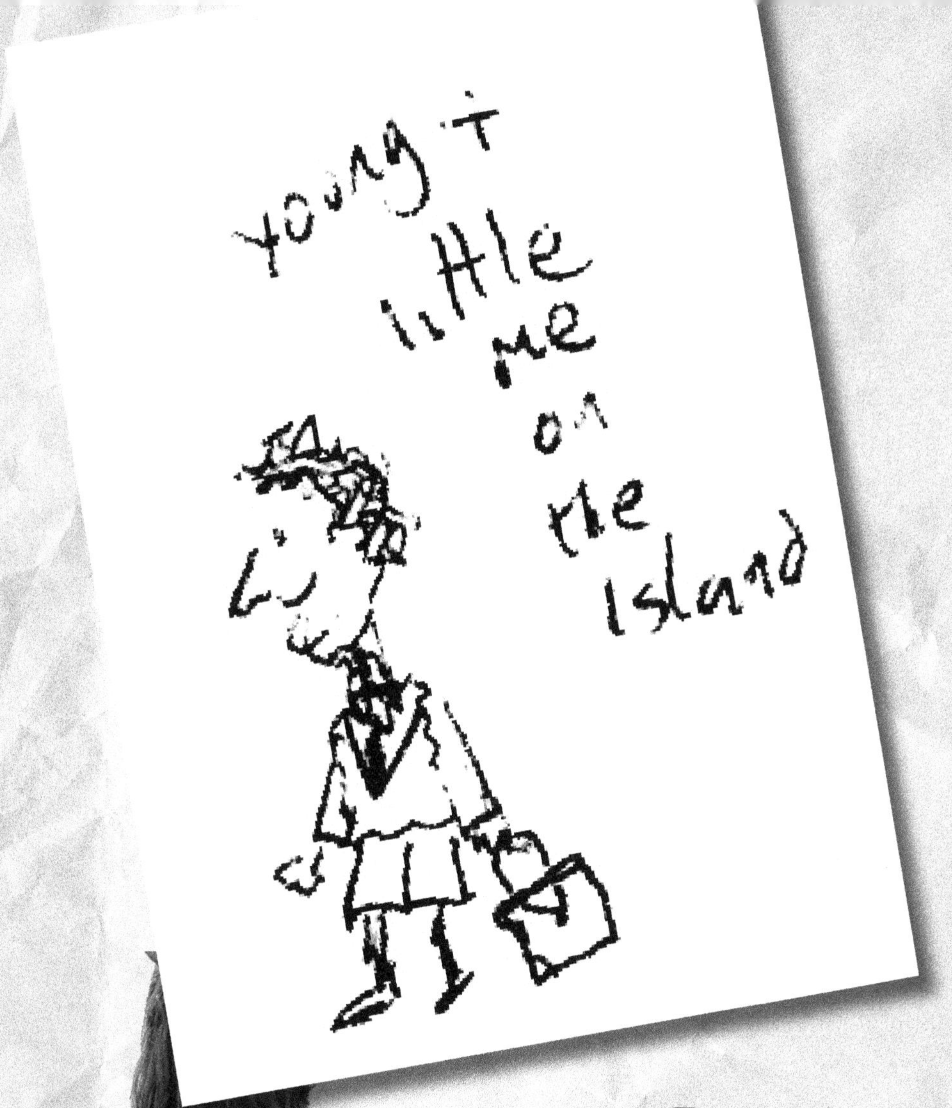

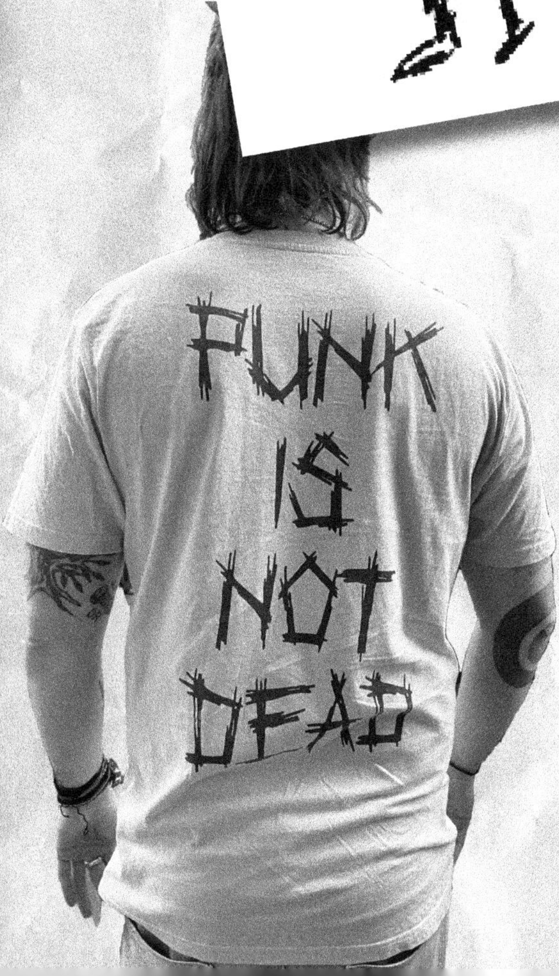

for Bea

contents

foreword by Jared Brown & Anistatia Miller • 9

preface by Eline Soo Yun Bosman • 13

introduction by Bea Bradsell • 15

chapter one

FROM THE BEGINNING • 16

chapter two

HOW FAR HAS THE BAR SCENE CHANGED? • 54

chapter three

A COCKTAIL DICKTIONARY • 64

chapter four

DICK'S COCKTAIL COURSE FOR BEGINNERS • 162

chapter five

WHERE WAS DICK? • 186

chapter six

LET YOUR FREAK FLAG FLY • 206

chapter seven

DICK'S MUSIC PLAYLIST • 218

epilogue by Dick Bradsell • 224

religion
is kindness

don't worry about it
it is a joke
be nice to people

THEME : LOOK AFTER YOUR
HEALTH + WELL BEING
KEEP FIT
KEEP FOCUSED
LIVE !

Desert = perception of the world
Cube = perception of the self
Stairs = Friends
glass = love
horse = desire

desert
cube stairs glass
horse

1 (A)

So why are you here then?
What made you decide on here?
There are two more - you had to pass to get here
So what do you like about it?
Ever asked yourself this? (surely yes)

You've decided to be a customer
Made a decision and now you are hooked
Waiting for delivery of your drink or
food.
Maybe you're seated with 'bev nap'
in front of you and a dish of snacks
within reach. That is quite a leap.
Did you have time to wait, a booking,
an appointment? Or had you just heard
of the place "word of mouth" and wanted
to try it out. I'm getting on the last
But maybe you just liked the look of the
place. It was welcoming. And what is that?
Welcoming ... : A smile. A legible and
enticing menu. Some samples of the fare
A table/a chair a clean table cloth A beckoning
arm. "A table for two?" "Have you booked?"
"Take a seat" And in you went Caught + expectant

foreword

DICK CALLED ONE AFTERNOON AND and said we needed to have lunch. A few days later, he and Eline sat across from us in a London sushi restaurant. "I want to open a bar with you two," he started. It was like Pélé saying he was putting together a five-a-side and wanted us as wings. There could only be one answer: Yes. We reached out to Mal Evans in Leeds. London needed a MOJO bar— one with a hidden bar inside, Dick's Bar. Dick said we would tend bar together a couple nights a week and leave the place to 'the kids' the rest of the time. He was already reaching beyond our wildest dreams. He was unquestionably among the world's top bartenders and bar mentors. He had so much more to share. He was just hitting *takumi*-level—a craftsperson who is unrivalled in their particular field of expertise.

Dick was a true master of the crafts of making drinks, taking care of guests, and running a bar day-to-day. Then Dick fell ill. The doctors thought it was epilepsy at first, but the truth was far worse and even harder to handle—incurable and terminal. The bar was for him and about him, and there was no thought of going forward without him.

Dick's creation, the Espresso Martini, is arguably the most popular drink invented in the last fifty years. But it is a bare fraction of his legacy as a bartender and mentor, and as the father of modern British bartending. Following are Dick's stories in his own words—in his own handwriting wherever possible. Here are the photos he collected of his life and throughout his life. Here are the recipes he created and illustrated. This book is his, assembled after the world lost him at age 57, but compiled by Dick with help from his loving partner Eline in the last year of his life. It arrived in binders and envelopes and scrapbooks—enough to fill two carry-on suitcases. It took years to arrange all the pieces.

Dick wanted his book on drink to resemble a classic cocktail volume, *Nip Ahoy*. If he had lived to handwrite and illustrate it, it would have been—except with far better content. (And if anyone out there has the time and talent and energy to pay respect to him with a graphic novel, we invite you dive in.) As it was, we reached back to the styles of the magazines that wrote about Dick, created by writers and editors and publishers who drank Dick's drinks, who loved him and loved his work. Dick was by his own admission a punk: a punk who shaped and was shaped by the birth of the London scene. Thus, magazines like the *FACE* and *ARENA* and even *Smash Hits* influenced the design of this book. But mostly, it was Dick's intensity, his energy and his style that gave life to these pages.

Dick always carried a reporter's spiral notepad. Frequently, when he created a new drink for a guest, he would write and illustrate the recipe and give it away—though putting scraps of paper in drunks' hands doesn't assure they will endure. Thankfully, many of those drinks, such as the Wibble, took on lives of their own and outlived those first pencil sketches. May this book stand testament to a life lived to the fullest.

—Jared Brown and Anistatia Miller

Got memories of Dick or one of his recipes to share?
Visit http://www.mixellany.com/dick-s-page.html

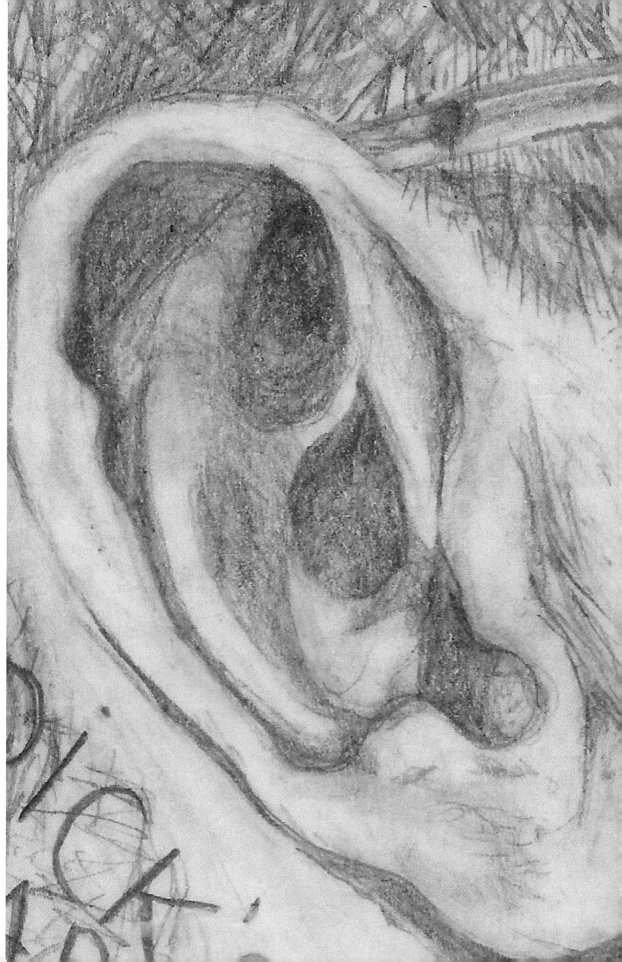

a book of dick: a preface

THIS IS THE LONG-AWAITED BOOK written by Mr. Dick Bradsell. AKA Soho Cocktail Legend, Father of the London Cocktail revival, The Bartenders' Bartender, Cocktail King, Creative Genius, are some of the titles attributed to him—though he would have introduced himself as Dick or perhaps Rosie Smudge or Cassandra the Wizard or Dungeon Master or…. His name is short for Richard, and with multiple Richards in the school yard, the nickname Dick was the only one left for him to choose. It stuck with him for the rest of his life.

It is not a cocktail book or a bar manual, because he believed that others were better at writing those than him. Although incomplete and missing the Author's final signature of approval and his inimitable voice, this book of thoughts, soundbites and (many) cocktails is part of his legacy that he had in life by way of reputation.

Compiled and carefully reconstructed from his own writings, his words (and his opinions) from his incalculable notebooks, personal letters, and scraps of paper span almost four decades are reproduced in the raw so all the feeling and emotion of his thoughts are left in their finest unedited, unpolished form. Photos from private collections and his own artwork are sprinkled throughout as playful as they appeared in his notebooks. This book is a tribute to his family and many friends who shaped his tread in life and supported him for better and for worse, in mind, spirit, and body. Ultimately, it is a celebration of the life and work of a proud British bartender, named Richard Arthur Bradsell.

So pour yourself your favourite drink and let Dick stroll you through his life!

—Eline Soo Yun Bosman

NILE CRUISE

DICK

introduction

BEFORE PROCEEDING WE RECOMMEND gathering the tools of every good bartender—3 pens, 2 lighters, and a waiter's friend. Dick Bradsell was an influence to so many and continues to be so; however to those who knew him he was so much more than the Espresso Martini or the Bramble. He was the party starter, matchmaker, anarchist, the inventive mind but beyond that he was the advisor, ally in your corner, shoulder you could always rely on, and the trusted ear.

How does one put into words the life of a character such as my father? In truth, it was a challenge that we only briefly fretted over as we quickly realised no one would be able to tell the story better than the man himself. Gathering his words and works were really the only option that made any sense.

In this book we welcome you to not just experience his creations (of which there were many) but also the surrounding elements that made up his full character.

—Bea Bradsell

FROM THE BEGI

Hello, my name is Richard Arthur Bradsell and I was born in Bishop Stortford, Hertforshire on May the 4th 1959. (I am told this is the Star Wars birthday "May The Fourth Be With You"? But it's a bit tenuous.) I share my birthday with a 6ft5in transsexual called Sybil Rouge but I am a lot older than her (I think) [did you know Miss Brighton was won by a man once?]. Funny old world innit!

When I was sharing my flat with a Jewish mystic lady, she asked me to find out my exact time of birth so she could produce/formulate a star chart of astrology. But when I asked my mum she said "I was busy at the time". I guess she was!

I was almost born in a bathroom at the hospital because they forgot my mum was having a bath and left her there. My mum said the first word I would have heard was "bitch" cos that is what she called the nurse. But my mum doesn't swear (she fucking well does, just not very often).

I grew up in East Cowes, on the Isle of Wight, off the South Coast of England, next to Queen Victoria's Osborne House, across the river from West Cowes; the UK's yachting centre. [listening to the fog horns late at night. And once to Jimi Hendrix's final concert, 25 miles away, literally shaking my window panes with his guitar in 1970?]

BTW: Jimi Hendrix's final concert took place on 31 August 1970 at the Isle of Wight Festival.

JESUS·SAID "SUFFER·THE·LITTLE·CHILDREN·TO·COME·UNTO·ME"
AND·FORBID·THEM·NOT·FOR·OF·SUCH·IS·THE·KINGDOM·OF·HEAVEN

HOLY BAPTISM

Name... Richard Arthur

The Child of ... Peter Beadwell and Margaret Elma Beadwell

Was Baptised on ... July 15th 19.. at St James' Church, East Cowes

Godparents ... Michael Ridley

... Timothy Waller

... Gladys Sandy ... Signed ...

✝ Ye are to take care that this Child be brought to the Bishop to be confirmed by him

19

Like a lot of UK catering folk I failed at school. I was a punk and foolish and failed to value education. I started washing up in hotels. I needed a better job and my parents sent me off to work for my uncle at the Naval and Military Club, the "In & Out", an old military and naval officers club on Piccadilly in London, opposite Green Park as a trainee assistant manager: Live in, £21.96 a week.

Photograph of
wife

EMPLOYMENT
DUCTIVITY
WES

EMPLOYMENT EXCHANGE

Signature of bearer
Signature du titulaire......Richard Bradsell

Signature of wife
Signature de sa femme.........

WARNING TO HOLDER

Before making a journey abroad with this passport you should
check that it is:—

(a) Still in force and will not expire before you return.
(b) Valid for the countries you propose to visit or travel
through (see page 3).

If in doubt contact your nearest Employment Exchange.

My mother was not looking at me. A bad sign. She was sitting, reading *She* magazine smoking a cig' and drinking Cinzano or Martini Dry and lemonade at our light blue Formica kitchen table whilst she waited for her patient visiting her surgery at our home. She was a medically-trained chiropodist. Why she was not looking at me was cos I had had a wild party at the house when the parents were away. Crashed my

THE STORY OF HOW THIS HAPPENED TITLED "THANK YOUS AND SLUGGINS" [THE IRONY OF NOT BEING ABLE TO INVENT A NEW GOOD COCKTAIL] (WITH ADDITIONAL SCENE)

sisters' allowed party. Redecorating had to take place (again).

"You are going to London to work for your uncle at The In and Out, The Naval and Military Club."

"What, Uncle Oscar? Evil Uncle Oscar?" [RIP]

"He prefers to be called Peter," she replied.

At least she was speaking to me.

THE 'FICTIONAL' SCENE

I am scared of doing things like this. Attending my interview. 20th of May 1977, 11:30 am, Fleet and Air Force Club Piccadilly. I had to meet Uncle Paul in a pub in Shepherds Market. I was half an hour early.

The pub had just opened but it already had a few men in various states of insobriety leaning at the bar. I got a coke. Mumbled at the camp bartender. Got confused with my money and my order. Was discounted as an idiot. Their conversation resumed.

I sat at a table and hoped the coke would not make me want to pee during the interview. I was wondering about visiting the pub facilities when my Uncle came in.

Tall with an eye patch and glasses. Grey pinstriped trousers and waist coat, white shirt, black tie and black jacket. A club manager's uniform. He was in off-duty mode.

"All right Nick. How are you mate?" "I am fine Uncle Paul" I said, carefully putting out my hand. "Never mind that." He said, grabbing me by the arm and dragging me to the bar. He seemed to know every one. They all scowled at him. He greeted them and bought a double vodka whilst waving a tenner. "What are you having Nick?"

"Er, I've got a coke over there" I said imply.

He looked confused staring at me for a couple of seconds.

"Make it two doubles. One with coke," he said carrying on and trying unsuccessfully to bum a fag.

END SCENE

HIS JOB WAS QUITE PRESTIGIOUS BUT A SERVANT OF SORTS. AND HE WAS A ROGUE.

"You have an interview with a Brigadier Walker next week. He runs the finances.

You meet your uncle at Waterloo at 2pm."

So we set about arranging my goods and chattels. New suit, pants, socks, fresh hankies, crisp + white plus new shirt (to me anyway) and several smart ties that were not school ties. My school ties were grubby and inauspicious.

We got a really cool 3-piece thin blue white striped suit from a charity shop plus a yellow button down collar shirt like Mick Jagger had. And with a mean thin tie.

Long with room to do a groovy knot.

I reckoned I looked both smart and….well cool I guess.

So the next week I set off from East Cowes, Isle of Wight for Portsmouth

and the train for London by the Wightlink Ferry. My new life was about to start.

Meet my uncle and go to the interview. He was easy to find at Waterloo. Tall with glasses. The "Gurney look". My mother's brother—very smartly dressed in a Gentleman Club's uniform, a morning suit like a wedding best man. Grey striped trousers, a black jacket. Smart shirt, waistcoat with chains and buttons – grey too and a cravat tie. All smacking of expense.

We got a taxi cab to Piccadilly, opposite Green Park. He went to make arrangements and do business in the club. The manager ranked number 3 there, Major Anderson superceded him, as did the financial director.

His job was quite prestigious but a servant of sorts. And he was a rogue. Sorry but he was. Do the opposite of what he said and you'd probably be on the right track!

The job I was up for was trainee assistant manager. I basically knew nothing. I had washed up glasses and dishes in kitchens in the South Coast hotels, Eastbourne etc.

I was here to learn. To learn everything. Bit by bit doing everyone's two weeks holidays. Trying to be useful. Get an education in the hospitality industry. Very green but willing. And, of course, my uncle had not

mentioned my relationship to him.

I was ushered through a highly polished brass stepped doorway into a reception past a switchboard with a bubbly and efficient receptionist [name forgotten] behind the scenes thru a side door where (as usual in the business) it all got a bit manky carpet and a bit drab to Brigadier Walker's office. He was a tanned man with pointy nose like mine, little glasses and eyes that scoured you. An army guy. No fool, certainly.

He shook my hand and introduced himself.

First question.

"Exactly what is your relationship to Mr Gurney?"

"Sir?" I replied.

"As in how does he know your mother?"

"He is my uncle sir, my mother's brother."

His next statement pended but pleased me.

"You've got the job. We'll give you a go."

"I like that you were honest" "I think your uncle will not. He kept that quiet."

I said "I really want to apply myself and learn here." "I think I have a lot to offer and I work hard and am diligent. I'm not afraid of getting stuck in. I hope you understand I have to be discreet and know my place and be secretive and keep my mouth shut."

Brigadier Walker (said) "...I do appreciate that. Very much. Your job will be to cover everyone else's holidays. So you've got to learn the lot! We have fixed ways here and you have to come up to scratch straight off. But we are used to teaching folk.

"You will have to learn a handshake. Yours isn't good enough. Sorry. Will be a lot of handshaking too. Hellos etc. with important folk. Major Anderson will teach you.

"I'll just go see him. Tell him, then introduce you."

Major Anderson ran the place with the help of the esteemed special police constable who worked reception at the grand entrance past the "In" and "Out" signs (hence the nickname), past the much needed car park at the front. Major Anderson grabbed my hand. He was about 60 something with wig like hair. Army turnout suit. No stinting on his clothing. Super smart shoes. Grabbed hand.

"One, two, three, shake. Thank you very much. That's it. Right every time. But don't kiss the hand. Ever. I hear you passed The Truth test. We checked you out. Welcome to the job Richard." He smiled reptileanly. I was pleased.

"You live in. We have staff rooms very top of the building. You get £21.96 a week. And don't hang out with the other staff. Can be quite a mixed lot. Especially the summer extras. And the hire ins for functions. To be frank, they steal stuff. The silver etc. You'll get duties every day. One will be to occasionally search the ladies in black and whites doing functions. Won't make you popular. Derek has to do it too. He runs the buttery. Old gay very camp. He'll teach you a lot. Cappuccinos, teas, espressos. Crumpets, buns. Toast as the members like it. On a tray in their way. Just be formal and friendly or pleasant you'll do."

IT WAS 1977, AN AWESOME YEAR IN LONDON HISTORY. I LEARNT EVERY ASPECT OF THE HOSPITALITY INDUSTRY AND CATERING TRADE IN JUST ONE YEAR.

It was 1977, an awesome year in London history. I learnt every aspect of the hospitality industry and catering trade in just one year. I worked everyone's holidays. Reception, switchboard, chamber maiding, table service. The making of classic drinks. Breakfast service. Goat room luncheon and Smoking Room duties. Function rooms service. Stock control and cleaning. A hell of a start. Silver service on day 3.

I was useless, thrown in the deep end. Ended up in the kitchen poisoning the poor members with my inept cooking until I learnt. Spoon round the back of the head style.

At the club they made Pink Gins. Where else would you get Pink Gins in the mid-70s?

I had to buckle down, learn how to make Pimm's, Martinis, gin and tonics.

I worked there for a year and went from being chef to do front of house. But I was paid so little. A lot of catering is slave labour, I went from there to train with a friend of my uncle's to be a chef, until I realised I'd much rather work front of house and meet people.

It's far more exciting.

30

ne Home Secretary presents his
ompliments and has the honour
o transmit the enclosed Defence
Medal which has been awarded
in recognition of service
during the war of
1939-45.

31

3,108,224

2 Sheets-Sheet

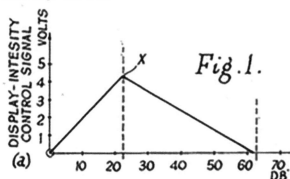

Fig.1.

INPUT

16

FIRST
DETECTOR

13

VIDEO
COMBINING

INVENTOR

Peter Bradsell

BY

Palmer & Stewart

ATTORNEY

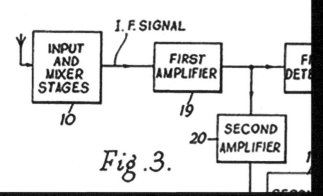

Fig .3.

"My father Peter Bradsell, a physicist and electrical engineer. A man who has done no harm. A man of great thought and principal, super intelligent from very young. Runs his life properly and with positive hope."—Taken from email interview in 2015 in which Dick was asked who were his role models

Fig.4.

DOWN AND OUT

IN HONG KONG AND LONDON

I left when my uncle did and started in the small kitchen of The Little Ship Club in the city of London. Then my flatmate's girlfriend Sophie Parkin got me a job as "the runner" (making coffees, bringing the waitresses the plated food, etc.) in the amazing Zanzibar Club. It was the perfect cocktail club. Based on a speakeasy's plan.

Full of actual celebrities like David Bowie, Catherine Deneuve, Elaine Paige, etc. I tried to make myself indispensable and loved the place. It was so glamorous. I was so shy. I made all my mistakes

EVERYONE HAS A FIRST DAY BEHIND A BAR!

early. Everyone has a first day behind a bar! My most formative experiences in my professional career... Well, they were the year at The Naval and Military Club, a great background and career "backbone" and training at the Zanzibar Club in the fine art of mixing drinks with Ray and

Pat. The senior bartender Ray Cook and the day bartender Pat Hassan taught me "the way of the bar". I tapped into a long line of drinks mixers.

I was very lucky. Pat's uncle had been senior bartender. Ray made me read *The Fine Art of Mixing Drinks* by David A Embury. And it was a lot more fun making drinks behind a bar than cooking in a kitchen with psychos. Instant gratification for your client. So, I guess bartending chose me.

IN THE CITY

RICHARD BRADSELL
CURRENTLY STAYING AT
11 DOMBEY HOUSE
HENRY DICKENS COURT
(HOLLAND PARK)
LONDON W11. but not for long

MR + MRS P. BRADSELL
HAZELWOOD
22 NEW BARN ROAD
EAST COWES
ISLE OF WIGHT
PO32 6AY.

WED 9TH MARCH 83

Dear Mum and Dad.

How are you? I'm still making arrangements to move into my new flat with Alistair. I've actually seen it now. It's a maisonette decorated in fashionable modern styles. Definetly a "Des. Res.". The only problem is my landlord will be Tony Mackintosh who is also the director of Zanzibar. At least he knows I can afford the rent (£35 a week!).

Our other plans are coming along fine too. That is the plans for our bar. We have decided that - maybe just as a "working-name" - we will call it "The Drinking Club".

We have looked at a few places, the best being the bottom of "The Pollo" Italian restaurant in Cambridge Circus. We have written to them and are now just hoping. Dominic keeps on trying to persuade me to go on what he calls "cocktail research". In fact we all did last night. We went to Trader Vics at the bottom of the Hilton and the Bar on the roof there, also the Beachcomber bar in Mayfair Hotel + the Ritz. You can guess which was the best - The Ritz - we knew it probably would be - All the drinks were excellent + reasonably priced there, especially their real real strawberry Daiquiris. I couldn't believe how awful all the other places were were over priced, weak drinks with vital mistakes especially Trader vic's which once had a good reputation.

We have endless amounts of bits of paper and forms from the Small Firms Service + Inland Revenue etc. (They seem to be doing good business!) We have decided that the place will be a club with no members. That means only people we let in can come in, and we have an excuse that will not offend people if we don't like the look of them.

The style will be mainly decided by the drinks. All cocktails, especially the TRADIONTAL ones   SOURS · DAIQUIRIS · MAI TAIS ETC made property to the best recipes (something I have a collection of) And also the more strange ones whoes makings have been lost to time (I've got a lot of old cocktail books - I checked your MRS BEATON too!) The main idea is that we are just cheaper + better + correct if that fails then there is something wrong with them not us.

All the people who are going to invest will be working there except one. She is called Liz and she will be in charge of getting all the "STARS" of the social circles to come. She has already helped because her husband (a rich painter) has been trying to open a restaraunt for a while   and he has given us tips on where to look. Funny that half of London's night life is owned by a few people such as PAUL (YEUCH) RAYMOND.

Ian has got a job as a head of his own bar in the revamped Piccadilly Theatre. I wish I could find a job. I suppose it would help if I looked - but I have always found my jobs on the grapevine of catering people. People in the trade have far better descriptions too, much more accurate in conditions + pay information. I'm told by Adam (remember him 😊)'s ex-girl friend that something good is opening in August. She has been hired to get staff.

The weather is a lot milder now isn't it. Have you heard from Traff? I haven't! John is a lot happier - I think because his girl friend has gone to a funeral up north. I'm still training with him.

        Lots of love
            Dick (your son) XX

How's Helen + greg + the cat?

(3B)

①

3b GOODWOOD HOUSE
17 BABBINGTON PATH
MID LEVELS
HONG KONG CENTRAL
HONG KONG.

Dear Mum and Dad

Gosh! I appear to
be in Hong Kong. Before travelling out there
were severe difficulties with both staff
and tickets — I think travel agents are all mental.
I had to spend a weekend finding a D.J. who
would be suitable and also willing to leave at
4 (3-2-1) DAYS notice, but we did. Then they
refused to give us our air tickets without
pre-payment. Soph' was already out there
here by that time so all manouveres had
to be performed on International phone lines
which was ridiculous.
The last few days we had to wait until 5 A.M
for a phone call from Hong Kong which would
tell us if we had a 10 AM flight!

I went out with Ian the others and a girlfriend to get drunk on Wednesday (or was it Thursday) and – whilst lying on some ones floor at about 12 noon – I got a desperate call from Ian that we left at 2 p.m. – Oh mi god.

The flight was the cheapest possible and went via Bombay (lovely place) and then on to Honkers Arrived half-insane [sarcasm] with the others. We went out that night and have had Jet-lag – which is so strange – ever since. Though I think I got sunstroke yesterday.

Our accomadation is o.k. or rather: will be o.k. when we rid ourselves of the waitresses (3) sharing the living room. They have been here 4 months and messed the place up quite a bit. Please write to the above address.

The club (NINETEEN 97) is half finished, very small, owned by a German, in dispute with the authorities and has a reputation for being a grotty place. This we will change.

② Our contract is for 3 months trial and then a further year. So if it doesn't work out I will return. I find myself rather ~~guarded~~ guarded about its prospects I don't really think that the owners know enough about catering - from what Sophie has told me.

Oh well it's a challenge and ~~I've~~ I've only been here two days.

Some friends of the overseer of the establishment took us on their company junk to an island with two restaurants on. (which is where I got sun stroke I think) They were the best seafood restaurants I've ever been too and the bill was 60 HK$ (six quid) each - that's expensive for here.

cotton sox 50p
Taxi anywhere 50p
lunch £1.00 etc.

In Hong Kong all internal phone calls are free but very expensive to the outside.

I hope this letter is legible but I'm very odd in the head still and drift off now and then with one of the many distractions around — jack - hammer - cockroach - funny bird noises — sudden rain etc.

There is a Typhoon here in two days so I'll be playing endless games of scrabble when you read this.

All my love

Dick (your son)

xxx

P.S. Hong Kong itself is nice - very hot and some people are quite friendly on trams and things especially the Indians

Bye

P.P.S. I'll write again when I am normal!

本署檔號 *OUR REF.:* (56) **in** HK/C/C 18/2 VI

來函檔號 *YOUR REF.:*

電話 *TELEPHONE:* 5-252345

內線 *EXTENSION:* 93

TELEX NO.: 65367 HX

Central Division,
Central Police Station,
10 Hollywood Road,
Hong Kong.

7 May 1986

Mr. & Mrs. Rand M.E. BRADSELL,

████████████████████

Dear Mr. & Mrs. Bradsell,

      I regret to inform you that we have been unsuccessful in locating your son, Mr. R.A. Bradsell who had apparently went back to U.K. sometime in August 1985.

      According to friends of his who frequent the 1997 Club, stated Richard was last seen in February this year working for a Club in Soho, London called the "Soho Brasserie", but he finished working there a month after.

      Attempts to find out his current whereabout to no avail. However, we should endeavour to let you know at first instance when we come up with further information.

(P.C. Burbidge-King)
Divisional Commander, Central
for Commissioner of Police

Dear Mum + Dad

Sorry I have been so cruel to you. I am a selfish little brat
I hope you can forgive me?

I managed to get out of Hong Kong by the skin of my teeth with my
pants on fire. Things will never be the same again, at least not in my
life. Ian and Sophie run away to Australia + Dominic + I returned via
Hawaii to regain our faith in humanity (it worked)
When I got back to London I had sweet FA and used to be in K. Porter
etc etc... but my very good friends rallied around and helped me out of the
mess I was in. It was time to grow up. Humility is a wonderful process for
the arrogant.

I now work in a really great job with nice people and have become
an artist of sorts. Sophie has bought a house in Hackney with her sensible
boyfriend — who rushed to Aussie land to save her — (I am going to live in
the basement with a garden and stuff. A permanent home! (a new experience)

If you can write to me I will be very grateful. Please be careful
as I am very vulnerable about you now. (I cry every whenever I think of you.

I am sorry. Truly.

All my love Dick (your Son) + still I hope

xxxx

I hope you are well.

MEETING
VICKI

①

Dick. A. Bradsell
150 Glenarm Road
Homerton
Hackney
London E5 0N3
18/12/86

Dear Mom and Dad,

Hope you are cheerful and that the preparations for christmas are going alright. I phoned Helen at work, after receiving a card, and she told me all the news. She sounds very optimistic and I felt quite cheered by her conversation. I am sorry that you haven't been well. I can't have been much help.

I am enjoying my job at the Moscow Club as the place has really taken off. Although the christmas trade in London has been low — I think people are buying presents rather than socializing — we have had some good nights. The club is a jolly family of friends which is most unusual for this cut throat catering industry.

I have fallen in love !!!

The lady in question is called Vicki Sarge and she is from Detroit Michigin. We have been seeing each other since the week before May when I met my

46

beloved at a party. She is the nicest person
I have ever met. On meeting her I was inspired
to write a poem on a coffee filter. It has
fairley knocked my life sideways as I have never
had a regular girlfriend (and very few irregular ones).

I'm sure we look and odd pair as she is quite
tall with long dark hair and I am a skinny little runt.

Helen said you are in the theatre now. Is that
the Apollo players? Dad is playing a singing reindeer
in the chorus?!? I thought London was wacky.

✗ We have been for several glorious holidays
and have founded a common interest in camping. Our
first jaunt was to the stunningly pretty Buttermere
in the Lake District - the week before they announced
that it was radioactivated by Chernobyl. We have a
two person tent made up from parts from our friends

off into the countryside. We have used the
British Tourist guides for campers which are
great. The quiet places They recommend
are the best we found. Next we went to
various spots in the Highlands which was quite cold
but almost as lovely.

    This weekend we spent a couple of days
in Brighton because Vicki is off to the States for
christmas & I plan to spend mine with a few friends
and an amiable Television — which I never get to watch
in my job.

    I now live in the basement of Sophie and her
boyfriend Alistair's house in Hackney which is most pleasant.
Soph is pregnant and I am going to move after January.
I suspect the child will be short + loud judging by the parents
but all babies are aren't they.

    I have taken up being an artist of sorts and

have had two joint exhibitions with a travelling gallery run by a friend. Sold out both times which was both suprising and encouraging. It is probably because I kept the prices low and my friends were buying the pictures. The work is coloured cartoons with oil pastel on various subjects. I was persuaded ~~to start them~~ by some close friends to start the venture. They said that I missed expressing myself in my life. It gave me much to think about when they were proved right.

I hope you will bear with me while I sort my life out. I am full of hope and a special kind of joy now that I have find love.

Please have a very merry Christmas and light a candle for me. I shall be thinking of you

Love Dick xxxx

"Now life has settled into a routine. He has lost a famously manic toothless grin by visiting a dentist and is now a family man. He met his wife Vicki at a notorious party in the All Saints Road three years ago which ended in blood and tears. Some journalists from Italian Vogue were taken on a tour of London's hippest parties. A fight broke out and the journalists had to be pushed into a fireplace to avoid people hitting each other with bottles. At some point during the battle, Bradsell met Vicki. 'It was a momentous meeting and love at first sight,' he says."—Andy Harris, Evening Standard, December 1989

CHAPTER TWO

HOW FAR HAS THE BAR SCENE CHANGED?

THE FANTASY OF FASHION.

GETTING DRUNK AND GLAMOUR. BUT IT WAS VERY "LOOKING FOR MR GOODBAR".

VERY FEW PLACES FOR THE ORDINARY DRINKER TO GO. APART FROM PUBS.

THE INTRODUCTION OF FRESH LIMES, CRANBERRY JUICE AND GOOD HAVANA RUM.

WIDENING OF COCKTAILS AWAY FROM THE USA [CHEERS AND "FERN BARS"], MEXICO, FRANCE, ITALY AND PERU, JAPAN. LONDON IN 1977 WAS SURPRISINGLY BORING.

1970s

PEOPLE FINDING PARTNERS FOR LIFE OR THE NIGHT OR JUST FINDING THE GUTTER [PRE AIDS].

THE RERELEASE OF THE SAVOY COCKTAIL BOOK AND THE FINE ART OF MIXING DRINKS.

LONDONERS HAD FUN. THEY KICKED OFF THE CHAINS OF THE PAST. LOTS OF WAREHOUSE PARTIES. HEDONISM.

THERE WAS A MINI COCKTAIL REVIVAL IN LONDON.

A REVOLUTION STARTED. PUNK, ROXY MUSIC, THE HUMAN LEAGUE, DAVID BOWIE.

HOW FAR HAS THE BAR SCENE CHANGED?

MOST PLACES DIDN'T HAVE A F***ING CLUE, SO WE FOUND THE PLACES THAT WERE MAKING GOOD COCKTAILS, THAT DID HAVE A CLUE.

BARTENDING AND CATERING GOT PROFESSIONAL AND GAINED PRIDE.

LIKE THE SAVOY: YOU DIDN'T JUST GO THERE FOR THE DRINKS, YOU WENT FOR THE ATMOSPHERE.

THE RITZ: THE GUY THERE WAS IN HIS 70S, MAYBE OLDER, HE WAS SO GOOD AT HIS JOB. HE MADE A GREAT STRAWBERRY DAIQUIRI, COPIED IT. HE WOULD EXPLAIN WHY IT WA[S] GOOD AND WHAT HE WAS DOING.

AND DUKE'S: AMAZING, YOU FELT YOU HAD WALKED OUT OF LONDON AND INTO SOMETHING REALLY GRAND.

CUSTOMERS BECAME EDUCATED VIA STYLE MAGAZINES AND WE GOT STYLE BARS.

IT SPREAD ACROSS THE UK. EDINBURGH, MANCHESTER OXFORD ETC. [THE UK ROD] THE FIRST STYLE BARS WERE UP NORTH AND SCOTLAND, THEY WEREN'T IN LONDON.

KEPT OUT THE WORKING MAN. WE MAYBE TOOK ON THE VALUES OF OUR PARENTS AND UNCLES.

UP THERE IT WAS A WAY OF KEEPING BUILDERS OUT. IN LONDON THEY JUST MADE BEER EXPENSIVE.

THE "E" GENERATION. LONDON ROCKED AFTER THE "SUMMER OF LOVE".

FILM FANTASY IN BAR CULTURE. THE COSMOPOLITAN. DESIGNER BEER. ABSOLUT VODKA. SHOTS AND SHOOTERS. PARTY TIME AGAIN

THE END OF BAR VIOLENCE [IT WAS A REAL PROBLEM!]

WE HAD A FINANCIAL CRASH BUT SOME STILL HAD THE MONEY. OR LET'S PRETEND WE ARE RICH.

ENGLISH PEOPLE THOUGHT IT OK TO SERVE SOMEONE. THE BUSINESS GUY WAS ICONIC. BUT IT WAS OK TO BE A SERVER. IT ACTUALLY BECAME A COOL JOB. TRAINING AND OLD SCHOOL VALUES.

1980s

HOW FAR HAS THE BAR SCENE CHANGED?

"CLUBBING" GOT TO BE AN ENTERTAINMENT. THE BAR SCENE GOT PROFESSIONAL. BARTENDERS OPENED THEIR OWN BARS. VERY GOOD TRAINING.

THE USE OF INTERNET COMMUNICATION TO SPREAD IDEAS. THE GOOD ROSE TO THE TOP.

THE BAR INDUSTRY AS SUCH TOOK OFF. PEOPLE SAW IT AS A WAY OF MAKING SERIOUS MONEY.

MANY NEW DRINKS + MANY NEW PRODUCTS. SUPPORT FROM LIQUOR OR SPIRIT COMPANIES IN BARS AND CHAINS.

SO MANY NEW BARS OF DIFFERENT TYPES. SIMON DIFFORD OF CLASS. THE TEAM AT THEME MAGAZINE. THE BAR SHOW. INTERNATIONAL BARTENDING.

1990s

BECAME A GOOD
PLACE TO MAKE A BUCK. BEFORE
FASHION AND CATERING WERE MOST
HIGH RISK VENTURES. WE STOPPED
LOOKING TO US FOR IDEAS AND LOOKED
TO EUROPE. WE GOT CONFIDENT.

I STARTED DOING
CONSULTANCIES AND
WE GOT PR
COMPANIES
TELLING US WHAT
TO DO.

HOW FAR HAS THE BAR SCENE CHANGED?

IT IS IMPORTANT TO BE POSITIVE. IT IS A NEW GENERATION.

THE RETURN OF TGI FRIDAYS STYLE FLAIR BARTENDING.

WE GET CULINARY COCKTAILS. NOT AS MUCH FUN. THE BARTENDER AS STAR. I PREFER TRADITIONAL VALUES BUT THAT IS ME.

IT ALL GOT A BIT MORE COMPARTMENTALIZED. HIDDEN SPEAKEASIES BEHIND COKE MACHINES. 1870S DRINKS. VERY OPINIONATED FIXED IDEAS. [YOU KNOW THE ZANZIBAR WAS A DIRECT COPY OF A SPEAKEASY'S PLANS!]

THERE ARE LOTS OF GREAT NEW PLACES AND I CAN'T WAIT TO SEE WHAT IS NEXT. EXCITING.

A LOT OF OUR BUSINESS RUN BY SOCIAL MEDIA: PR. "YOU DIDN'T EXCEED OUR EXPECTATIONS". THE BLIGHT OF THE CUSTOMER REVIEW.

THE BAR SCENE NOW (2015)

I LOVE A LOT OF THE NEWEST ONES. BRAVE NEW WORLD. LOTS OF GREAT SPIRITS AND LIQUEURS AND QUALITY STUFF. NEW GINS AND BAR DISTILLING ETCETERA, MORE KNOWLEDGE AND TRAINING.

MORE HISTORY! MORE MYTHS AND INACCURACIES! BUT THAT'S THE WORLD OF COCKTAILS!

A COCKTAIL

Here are 131 of Dick's drink recipes...

CHAPTER THREE

DICKTIONARY

DICK'S COCKTAILS FROM HIS TAKES ON CLASSICS AND CONTEMPORARIES TO DICK'S OWN VERSIONS OF HIS OWN

ALEXANDER
AMARETTO SOUR
AMERICANO
AVIATION
BACARDI COCKTAIL
BLACK RUSSIAN
BOURBON SOUR
BRANDY ALEXANDER
CADILLAC MARGARITA
CAIPIRINHA
CLASSIC MARGARITA
CLOVER CLUB
COFFEE CHASER
DARK & STORMY
DRY MARTINI
GIMLET
GIN+IT/GIN MANHATTAN
HARLEM DRY GIN MARTINI
HARLEM VODKATINI
HARVEY WALLBANGER
HOT BUTTERED RUM
HOT WINE PUNCH
JUNEBUG COCKTAIL
KUMQUAT & ALMOND
CAIPIRINHA

MARTINIS
MARY PICKFORD
MONKEY GLAND
MOSCOW MULE
NEGRONI
NEW YORK SOUR
OLD FASHIONED
PING PONG
PISCO SOUR
RAFFLES GIN SLING
RAMOS GIN FIZZ
SCORPION PUNCH
SIDECAR
SING SONG
SLOE GIN FIZZ
SMOKEY MARTINI
THE STINGER
STRAWBERRY CAIPIRINHA
SWEET MANHATTAN
SWEET MARTINI
TOM COLLINS
VESPER
VODKA GIMLET
ZOMBIE

Want more recipes? Head to http://www.mixellany.com/ dick-s-page.html or click the QR code. We'll be adding more to this list until we publish Dicktales 2. Stay tuned.

ALEXANDER   (ARCHAIC?) SHAKE

GIN
LIGHT CACAO   COCKTAIL
CREAM   GLASS
ICE SHAKE + STRAIN
DUST WITH NUTMEG ?

BRANDY ALEXANDER   SHAKE

ANDER'S SISTER ETC

25 MLS   COGNAC
20 MLS   DARK CACAO
20 MLS   LIGHT CACAO
30 MLS   CREAM
                      CREAM
SHAKE WITH ICE AND STRAIN   COCKTAIL
                            GLASS
GRATE NUTMEG OVER DRINK

TRY WITH DARK OR GOLD RUM (RUM + TIA MARIA + CREAM)
KAHLUA INSTEAD OF CACAO

This first Brandy Alexander on your left uses cognac and adds more liqueur than the second one below.

BRANDY ALEXANDER   SHAKE

35 MLS   BRANDY
15 MLS   DARK CACAO
10 MLS   LIGHT CACAO
25 MLS   FRESH CREAM
SHAKE AND STRAIN
INTO COCKTAIL GLASS
GARNISH : GRATED NUTMEG

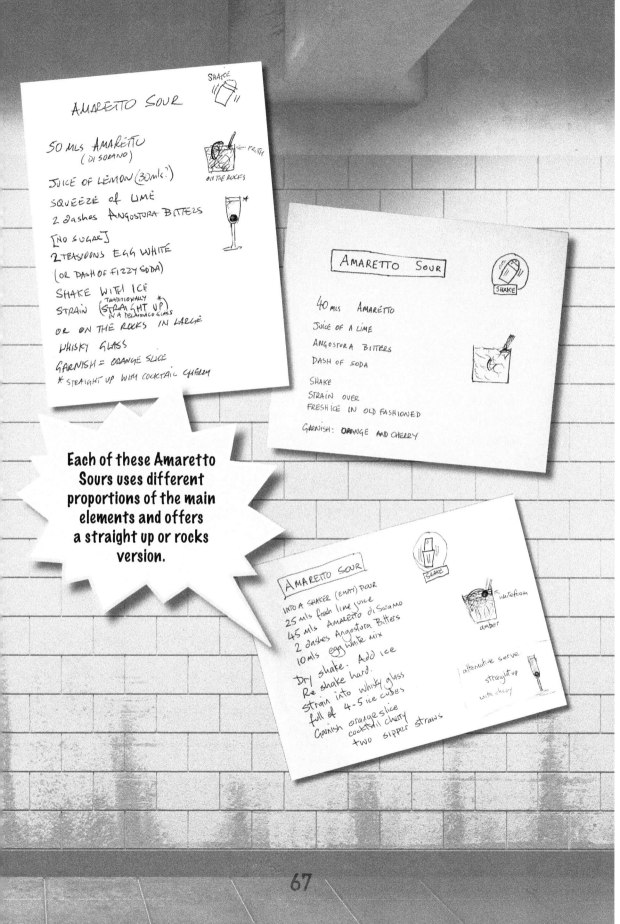

AMARETTO SOUR

SHAKE

50 MLS AMARETTO
(DI SORANO)

JUICE OF LEMON (30mls?)

SQUEEZE of LIME
2 dashes ANGOSTURA BITTERS

[NO SUGAR]
2 TEASPOONS EGG WHITE

(OR DASH OF FIZZY SODA)

SHAKE WITH ICE
STRAIN (STRAIGHT UP *) TRADITIONALLY IN A DELMONICO GLASS

OR ON THE ROCKS IN LARGE

WHISKY GLASS

GARNISH = ORANGE SLICE
* STRAIGHT UP WITH COCKTAIL CHERRY

← FROTH
ON THE ROCKS

*

AMARETTO SOUR

SHAKE

40 MLS AMARETTO

JUICE OF A LIME

ANGOSTURA BITTERS

DASH OF SODA

SHAKE
STRAIN OVER
FRESH ICE IN OLD FASHIONED

GARNISH: ORANGE AND CHERRY

Each of these Amaretto
Sours uses different
proportions of the main
elements and offers
a straight up or rocks
version.

AMARETTO SOUR

SHAKE

INTO A SHAKER (EMPTY) POUR
25 mls fresh lime juice
45 mls AMARETTO di Sorano
2 dashes Angostura Bitters
10 mls egg white mix

Dry shake. Add ice
Re-shake hard.
Strain into whisky glass
full of 4-5 ice cubes
Garnish orange slice
cocktail cherry
two sipper straws

white foam
amber

alternative serve.
straight up
with cherry

AMERICANO

BUILD

INTO A TALL GLASS
FULL OF ICE
POUR
25 MLS CAMPARI
25 MLS ROSSO
TOP WITH SODA
STIR
GARNISH: ORANGE +
LEMON SLICE
+ STRAW

The first Aviation uses less crème de violette than the one below it and calls out the brand used to make it.

'Rosso' means sweet red vermouth

AVIATION, THE

50ml Beefeater gin
25ml lemon juice
15ml Maraschino liqueur
5ml creme de violette
Ice
cherry

SHAKE

AVIATION

INTO A SHAKER FULL OF ICE POUR
25 mls lemon juice
45mls gin
20 mls Maraschino liqueur
[10mls creme de violette]

SHAKE AND STRAIN INTO PRECHILLED
COCKTAIL GLASS

GARNISH COCKTAIL CHERRY

SHAKE

opaque white
[azure, light purple]

BALARDI COCKTAIL
(AKA PINK DAIQUIRI)

SHAKE

A   DAIQUIRI

PINK

COCKTAIL
GLASS

MADE WITH GRENADINE
INSTEAD OF SUGAR SYRUP

{ GRENADINE   1½
  LIME   2   PARTS
  RUM (BACARDI) ᴬᴳᴱᴰ 6

I CANT WAIT

BLACK RUSSIAN

BUILD

POUR OVER ICE IN OLD FASHIONED
GLASS
40 mls VODKA
20 mls KAHLUA
STIR
GARNISH: ORANGE SLICE

BOURBON SOUR

INTO A SHAKER GLASS FULL OF ICE POUR

50 MLS WOODFORD RESERVE BOURBON

40 MLS FRESH LEMON JUICE

20 MLS SUGAR SYRUP

2 DASHES ANGOSTURA

(2 BARSPOONS EGG WHITE)

SHAKE AND STRAIN INTO OLD FASHIONED /WHISKY GLASS

GARNISH = LEMON + COCKTAIL CHERRY

WHISKY/
OLD FASHIONED
GLASS

SHAKE

THE INNER GRUMBLE

CAIPIRINHA

CHOP A LIME (OR HALF A BIG ONE)
POUR IN ½ AS MUCH SUGAR SYRUP
AS JUICE (OR BROWN OR WHITE
GRANULATED SUGAR ∴)
MUDDLE

STRAWBERRY CAIPIRINHA

Muddle

3 STRAWBERRIES
A WHOLE LIME
15ml sugar syrup
15ml Fraise liqueur
50ml Sagatiba cachaca
crushed ice

KUMQUAAT + ALMOND CAIPIRINHA

MUDDLE
4 × KUMQUAAT chopped
½ WHOLE LIME chopped

20mls ORGEAT
DASH ORANGE FLOWER WATER

1 SCOOP CRUSHED
50mls CACHACA (SAGATIBO)

CHURN 10 SECS
MORE CRUSHED
GARNISH 2½s KUMQUAAT

opaque white

CLOVER CLUB/CLOVER LEAF

50 mls   BEEFEATER GIN
25 mls   LEMON JUICE
15 mls   RASPBERRY SYRUP
10 mls   EGG WHITE MIX
  5 raspberries
(a mint leaf)

SHAKE

deep pink

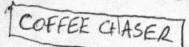

COFFEE CHASER

25 mls GRAND MARNIER
25 mls TIA MARIA
A COFFEE (HOT)
5 mls SUGAR SYRUP
35 mls CREAM
Cinammon

6
Pour

black + white

DARK + STORMY   ← from BERMUDA

50 mls MYERS
15 mls sugar syrup
25 mls FRESH LIME

ANGOSTURA   4 drops
TOP GINGER BEER
Garnish LIME WEDGE

Now, according to global trademark rules if you call this drink a 'Dark 'n'Stormy™' it has to contain Gosling's rum. If you do this Dick's way...

GIMLET

35mls BEEFEATER GIN
35mls ROSES LIME CORDIAL
1/4 OF A LIME
(ICE)

SHAKE

Pale green
cocktail glass

VODKA GIMLET

35ml WYBOROWA VODKA
35ml ROSES LIME CORDIAL
1/4 OF A LIME
(ICE)

Cocktail
glass

'GIN + IT' / GIN MANHATTAN

50 MLS BEEFEATER GIN
25 MLS MARTINI ROSSO
2 dashes Angostura bitters
cherry on a stick
orange twist

STIR

GOD FATHER

INTO A ROCKS GLASS FULL OF ICE POUR
50 ML J+B WHISKY
25 ML AMARETTO
STIR.
GARNISH = CHERRY + STIRRER

What is in a name?

Hi Dick BRADSELL HERE, Recently I have been
Rather ill (critically) But I bumped into Simon and his excellent
Partner / business partner Paloma and they had
reprinted an article from CLASS. to Difford's Guide
and asked if I might write some more? So here goes...

I am not often "boggled" [dictionary: perplexed, confused
not understanding] But this drink has done so. So much
so that I contacted a Cocktail Historian Anastasia
Miller but was left even more boggled, Here is the drink
(she mentioned it may be ~~Gilt~~ called a Martinez)

50 ml gin
25 ml Red (Italian?) Vermouth
dashes Bitters
on ice → Stirred, strained,
      prechilled glass.
      cherry on a stick

glass type   cocktail
            Nick + Nora

STIR

In my book it is either
A sweet Martini (Embury, Fine art of ...)
A "Gin and It" (or is it?) ⟶ (Gin sweet Vermouth equal parts)
A Gin Manhattan?

No wonder such a great drink
is little ordered. We don't know it's name
and doubt leads to mistakes.
But still I'd reccommend it
especially with a fine vermooth and gin
and a small spoon of cherry juice
Plenty of scope for adjustment ——— ☺

DB 25/5/2015

HARVEY WALLBANGER

INTO TALL GLASS FULL OF ICE
POUR
50 MLS VODKA

TOP WITH ORANGE JUICE
AND FLOAT 20 MLS GALLIANO

GARNISH: ORANGE SLICE, CHERRY
ON COCKTAIL STICK

HOT BUTTERED RUM

TWO
DASHES ANGOSTURA BITTERS
50 MLS MYERS RUM
25 MLS LEMON JUICE
10 MLS SUGAR SYRUP
50 mls pressed apple juice
KNOB OF BUTTER
HOT WATER
CINNAMON GARNISH

HOT WINE PUNCH

25 MLS LEMON JUICE
15 MLS sugar syrup
10 MLS CASSIS
5 MLS COINTREAU
1/2 glass house red wine
lemon slice
orange slice
nutmeg
cinnamon
cloves
HOT WATER

STIR

HEAT

JUNE BUG

1 measure bananas
1 measure malibu
1 measure midori
4 measures pineapple juice
1 measure lime juice

MARTINI   DERIVATIONS / TYPES / STYLES

FRANKLIN = A MARTINI WITH TWO COCKTAIL OLIVES
GIBSON   = A MARTINI WITH TWO COCKTAIL ONIONS

BUCK EYE = A MARTINI WITH A BLACK OLIVE

DIRTY = SHAKE WITH CRUSHED OLIVE + 2 BARSPOONS OF BRINE

007 / JAMES BOND = SHAKEN VODKA MARTINI + OLIVE ON STICK

NAKED = FROZEN GLASS, DASH OF VERMOUTH, FROZEN VODKA
(OR GIN) STRAIGHT FROM FREEZER
NO STIRRING NO SHAKING

"SEE THRU" = VODKA MARTINI ON THE ROCKS (NO VERMOUTH?)
(ALSO KNOWN AS GLASS OF VODKA?)

FRANKLIN   AFTER FRANKLIN D ROOSEVELT (US PRESIDENT) AND
MAKER OF BAD MARTINIS?

GIBSON   AFTER CHARLES DANAH GIBSON   ILLUSTRATOR
(DREW LARGE BREASTED COLLEGE GIRLS AT TURN
OF THE CENTURY (18c ⇒ 19c)]

Harlem Vodkatini

DASH OF MARTINI DRY VERMOUTH
(OR NOILLY PRAT DRY VERMOUTH)
INTO A SHAKER GLASS FULL OF ICE

STIR   STRAIN OFF LIQUID

ADD   60 MLS VODKA   (FINLANDIA)
(UPSELL = KETEL ONE / GREY GOOSE / BELVEDERE)

STIR AND STRAIN INTO CHILLED MARTINI GLASS

GARNISH = OLIVE   PITTED GREEN
                         NO PIMENTO

OR   = TWIST   THIN SLICE THUMB NAIL SIZED
                         OF LEMON PEEL
                         SPRAY OIL INTO GLASS AND WIPE
                         AROUND RIM OF GLASS

MAKE SPEEDILY
SERVE IMMEDIATELY

Harlem   Dry Gin Martini

DASH OF DRY VERMOUTH
(MARTINI DRY OR NOILLY PRAT)
INTO A SHAKER GLASS FULL OF ICE

STIR STRAIN OFF LIQUID

ADD 60 MLS   BOMBAY SAPPHIRE GIN
(UPSELL = HENDRICKS, MILLERS, TANQUERAY 10)

STIR AND STRAIN INTO CHILLED MARTINI GLASS

GARNISH = OLIVE OR TWIST

STIR

STIR

MARY PICKFORD

50mls HAVANA CLUB 3yo
25mls pineapple juice
15mls grenadine
Fresh pineapple
pineapple wedge
ice

SHARE

pink

Monkey Gland

1 1/2   gin

1 1/2   fresh orange

1 teaspoon real grenadine

1 teaspoon absinthe

shake

MOSCOW MULE

INTO A SHAKER FULL OF ROCK ICE POUR

50ml VODKA
25ml LIME JUICE

SHAKE   STRAIN OVER ICE
IN A   TUMBLER

TOP WITH GINGER BEER
GARNISH LIME WEDGE — TWO STRAWS

NEGRONI

STIR

INTO A PITCHER FULL OF ICE
POUR
30 MLS GIN
30 MLS MARTINI ROSSO
25 MLS CAMPARI
(OPTIONAL DASH ANGOSTURA BITTERS)

STIR THEN STRAIN OVER
FRESH ICE IN OLD FASHIONED GLASS
GARNISH : CHERRY, LEMON, ORANGE.

[CAN BE SERVED STRAIGHT UP
WITH LEMON TWIST

OR LONG ON THE ROCKS
WITH SODA

NEW YORK SOUR

SHAKE

35 mls MAKER'S MARK
bourbon
25 mls lemon juice
10 mls sugar syrup
Dash angostura bitters
10 mls egg white
25 mls Malbec red wine
float

We may never know which drinks got an X or a check or nothing. Only the cover was left.

sauceguide® TO COCKTAILS

MORE THAN 1,000 ILLUSTRATED COCKTAIL RECIPES INCLUDING: ...ATION, B-52, CAIPIRINHA, ...DAIQUIRI, ...ARITA, ...BIE...

POUR

OLD FASHIONED

STIR

INTO A WHISKY GLASS POUR

2 BARSPOONS SUGAR SYRUP (OR MUDDLE 2 SUGAR CUBES + WATER)
2 DASHES ANGOSTURA
3 ICE CUBES
STIR
ADD 25ML BOURBON
MORE ICE
STIR
ADD 25ML BOURBON
MORE ICE
STIR
MORE ICE
STIR
GARNISH: ORANGE TWIST

PING PONG

50mls SLOE GIN
25mls MARTINI ROSSO
2 dashes Angostura bitters
cherry on a stick
orange twist - ice

STIR

PISCO SOUR

50mls PISCO 1615
20mls lemon
10 mls lime
15mls sugar syrup
10mls egg white
garnish: angostura drops

SHAKE

RAFFLES GIN SLING

SHAKE

50 mls Beefeater gin
25 mls LIME JUICE
15 mls COINTREAU
Angostura bitters
20 mls CHERRY HEERING
50 mls pineapple juice
ginger beer
ice lime pineapple slice

pink

RAMOS GIN FIZZ

SHAKE

50 mls BEEFEATER gin
25 mls lemon juice
15 mls sugar syrup
35 mls cream
15 mls egg white
3 dashes orange flower water
soda water
(lemon wheel / cherry)

white

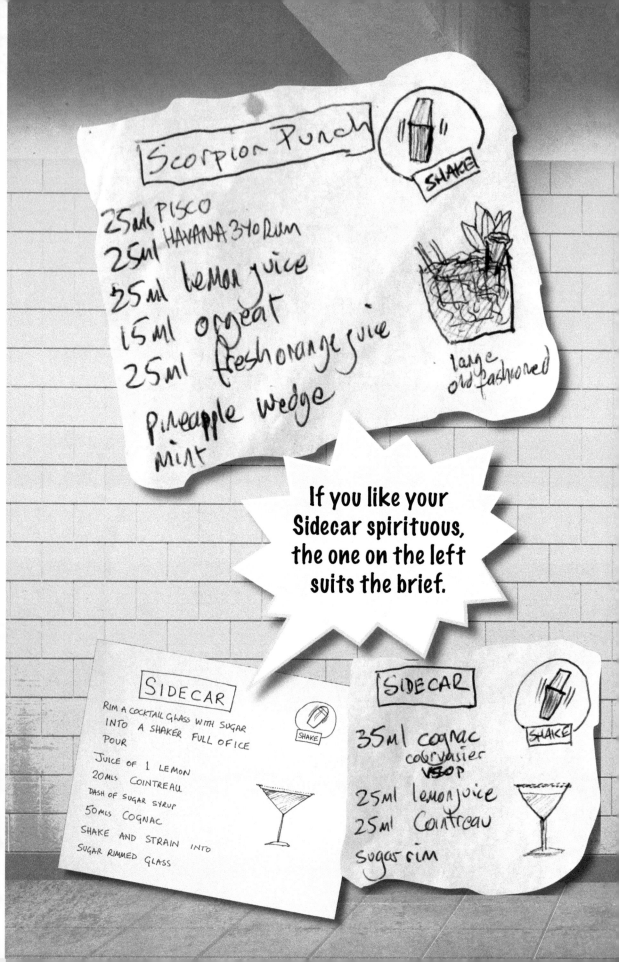

SLOE GIN FIZZ

10ml eggswhite Gordon's
50mls sloe gin

25mls lemon juice

15mls sugar syrup

Dash orange bitters

soda water

cherry / lemon slice

SHAKE

Purple/
white foam

Gin Martini
Negroni
White Lady
Singapore Sling
South side ▥
Bramble
Clover Club/Leaf
Aviation *
French 75
Ramos Gin Fizz
Tom Collins
Pegu Club *
Army + Navy *
The Gimlet

10
classic
gin
cocktails

Halifax, HX1 1WB

STINGER, THE

50ml cognac
15ml crème de
menthe, blanc
ice

SHAKE
A LOT

very cold

SING SONG

SINGAPORE SLING
INTO A SHAKER FULL OF ICE POUR
50mls BOMBAY SAPPHIRE GIN
35 mls LEMON JUICE
25 mls CHERRY HEERING
15 mls SUGAR SYRUP
SHAKE STRAIN OVER FRESH ICE IN DANGEROUS GLASS

TOP WITH SODA

STIR

GARNISH = LEMON + ORANGE 'BUTTERFLY' CHERRY TWO STRAWS

Tom Collins

INTO A SHAKER FULL OF ROCK ICE

50ML BOMBAY SAPPHIRE GIN
35ML FRESH LEMON JUICE
15ML SUGAR SYRUP

SHAKE STRAIN INTO DANGEROUS GLASS
FULL OF ICE
TOP WITH SODA
STIR
GARNISH = LEMON SLICE + CHERRY + TWO STRAWS

VESPER, THE

35ml WYBOROWA vodka
25ml Beefeater gin
15ml LILLET BLANC
1 drop Angostura bitters

STIR
SHAKE

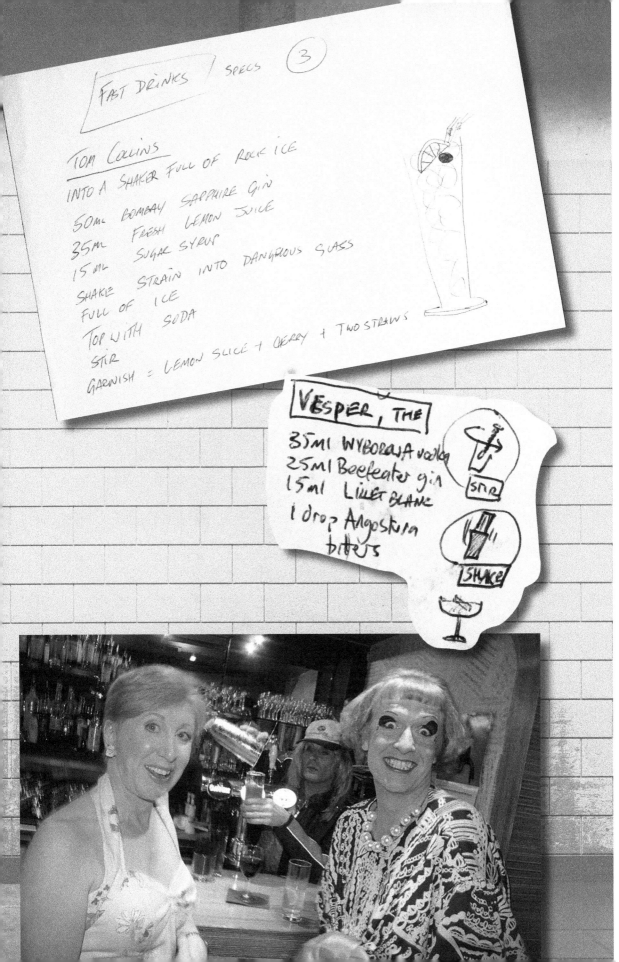

ZOMBIE
KILLER ZOMBIE

POUR OVER ROCKS IN "ZOMBIE
GLASS"   25ML LIME
GRENADINE
COINTREAU / CURACAO
VARIOUS RUMS (ESPECIALLY OVERPROOF)
ALL LAYERED
WITH SUGAR ON SURFACE
DRINK THRU STRAW
= EXOTIC GARNISH
(SHOULD BE 50 TO 75 MLS OF RUMS
INCLUDING OVERPROOF)

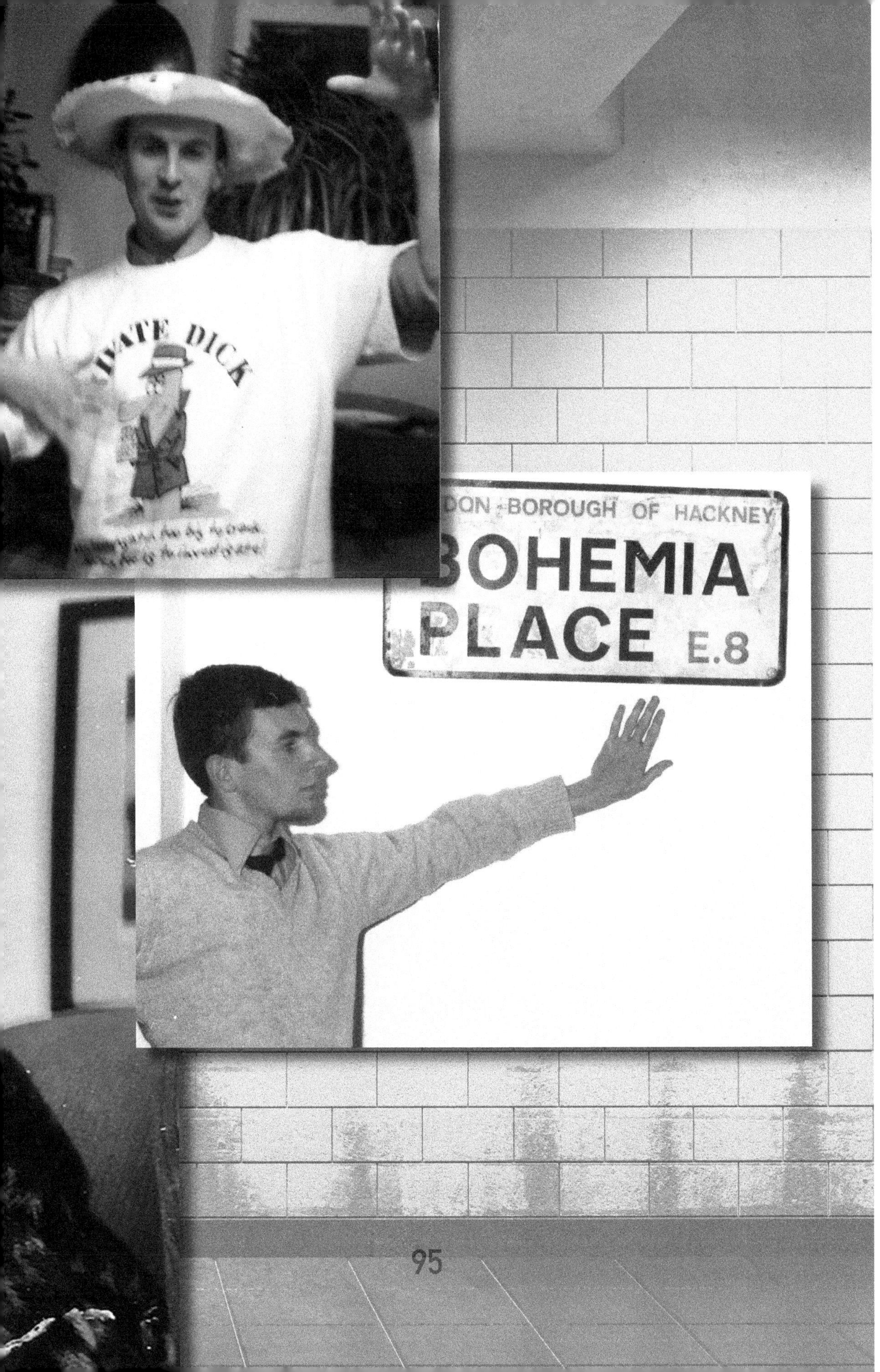
IVATE DICK
DON BOROUGH OF HACKNEY
OHEMIA
PLACE E.8

BAHIA

INTO A SHAKER FULL OF ROCK ICE POUR

50 ml HAVANA 3 year old RUM
75 ml COCONUT WATER
100 ml PINE APPLE JUICE
15 ml COCONUT SYRUP

SHAKE STRAIN OVER FRESH ROCKS
IN A TALL GLASS
GARNISH CHERRY + PINEAPPLE

CHOCOLATE BATIDA

blend

50 ml SAGATIBA CACHAÇA
35 ml CHOCOLATE SYRUP
15 ml DARK CACAO
25 ml CONDENSED MILK
5 ml SUGAR SYRUP

crushed ice

GARNISH:
CHOCOLATE POWDER RIM
A STRAWBERRY

dark brown
tumbler

CHOCOLATE MARTINI

STIR

50 mls WYBOROWA VODKA
20 mls LIGHT CACAO
5 mls WHITE MENTHE

CHOCOLATE + SUGAR RIM
pre-chilled cocktail glass

clear

26 · CONTEMPORARY

BAHIA
CHOCOLATE BATIDA
CHOCOLATE MARTINI
COSMOPOLITAN
ELDERFLOWER MARTINI
GOLDEN DRAGON
HONG KONG FUEY
LONG BEACH ICED TEA
LYNCHBURG LEMONADE
MARGARITAS
MARQUEE
NORTH SEA BREEZE
PASSION FRUIT MOJITO
QUIET STORM
THE RASPBERRY MARTINI
RASPBERRY MULE
RUSSIAN BRIDE
TATANKA
TEQUILA OLD FASHIONED
VANILLA DAIQUIRI

Now, you could call some of these contemporary drinks classics. But we guess we'll wait another decade or two before we call them true classics.

COSMOPOLITAN

35 MLS LEMON VODKA
25 MLS CRANBERRY
20 MLS COINTREAU
DASH ORANGE BITTERS
15 MLS LIME JUICE
DASH LIME CORDIAL

SHAKE OVER ICE
STRAIN INTO COCKTAIL GLASS

GARNISH: 'FLAMED' ORANGE TWIST

SHAKE

ELDERFLOWER MARTINI

SHAKE

INTO A SHAKER FULL OF ICE

SQUEEZE A WHOLE LIME

ADD SAME AMOUNT OF
ELDERFLOWER CORDIAL

40 MLS VODKA

SHAKE, STRAIN OVER INTO

FROZEN COCKTAIL GLASS

GARNISH: LIME TWIST

GOLDEN DRAGON

SHAKE

35 mls ALTOS REPOSADO TEQUILA

20 mls LIME JUICE

15 mls PISANG AMBON

100 ML CONCENTRATED APPLE JUICE

10 mls PASSION FRUIT SYRUP

orange rind

(ice)

HONG KONG FUEY

SHAKE

15 mls vodka wyborowa

15 ml beefeater gin

15 mls Altos blanco tequila

15 mls Havana Club 3yo rum

15 mls lime juice

10 mls Midori

10 mls Pisang Ambon

50 mls lemonade

lime slice
lemon slice
shaved

LONG BEACH ICED TEA

AS LONG ISLAND "
KAHLUA (not T/SEC)
CRANBERRY (not coke)

LYNCHBURG LEMONADE

INTO A SHAKER FULL OF ICE POUR
50mls JACK DANIELS
25mls LEMON JUICE
SHAKE, STRAIN OVER ICE IN A TUMBLER
TOP WITH LEMONADE
GARNISH LEMON SLICE, CHERRY — TWO STRAWS

TOMMY'S MARGARITA

SHAKE

(no salt!)

INTO A SHAKER FULL OF ICE POUR

45 MLS	ALTOS BLANCO TEQUILA
25 MLS	FRESH LIME JUICE
25 MLS	AGAVE MIX (HALF AGAVE SYRUP / HALF WATER)

SHAKE AND POUR ALL INTO CLEAR TUMBLER

GARNISH : LIME WEDGE
TWO 'SIPPER' STRAWS

(clear tumbler)

ALTERNATIVE SERVE:

straight up
(no ice)

(cocktail glass)

CADILLAC MARGARITA

SHAKE

(no salt!)

45 MLS	ALTOS REPOSADO TEQUILA
25 MLS	FRESH LEMON JUICE
25 MLS	GRAND MARNIER

SHAKE WITH ICE
POUR ALL INTO CLEAR TUMBLER

GARNISH : ORANGE SLICE
LEMON SLICE
TWO SIPPER STRAWS

(clear tumbler)

ALTERNATIVE SERVE!

straight up:
(no ice)

lemon slice

cocktail glass

CLASSIC MARGARITA

SHAKE or

BLEND

45 MLS ALTOS BLANCO TEQUILA

25 MLS FRESH LIME JUICE

25 MLS CARTRON TRIPLE SEC

DASH OF SUGAR SYRUP

SHAKE WITH ICE

POUR ALL INTO SALT RIMMED TUMBLER

GARNISH : LIME WEDGE
        TWO 'SIPPER' STRAWS

(clear tumbler)

Q: SALT OR NO SALT ?

[ON ROCKS ?
STRAIGHT UP ?
BLENDED ?]

ALTERNATIVE SERVE !

STRAIGHT UP
(no ice)
(cocktail glass)

BLENDED / FROZEN

(blended with crushed ice)

(new orleans tumbler)

"SILVER COIN" MARGARITA

SHAKE

45 Mls THEIR [YOUR] CHOICE OF TEQUILA

25 mls FRESH LIME JUICE

25 Mls COINTREAU

SHAKE WITH ICE

POUR ALL INTO TUMBLER WITH SALT RIM

GARNISH: LIME + LEMON WEDGE
        TWO 'SIPPER' STRAWS

(clear tumbler)

Q. SALT OR NO SALT !

[ON ROCKS
  STRAIGHT UP?]

ALTERNATIVE SERVE !

STRAIGHT UP
(NO ICE)

(cocktail glass)

HIBISCUS MARGARIITA
50 mls ALTOS PLATA TEQUILA
30 mls HIBISCUS SYRUP
20 mls LIME JUICE
15 mls AGAVE MIX
SHAKE DOUBLE STRAIN
GARNISH DRIED
HIBISCUS FLOWER

cranberry pink

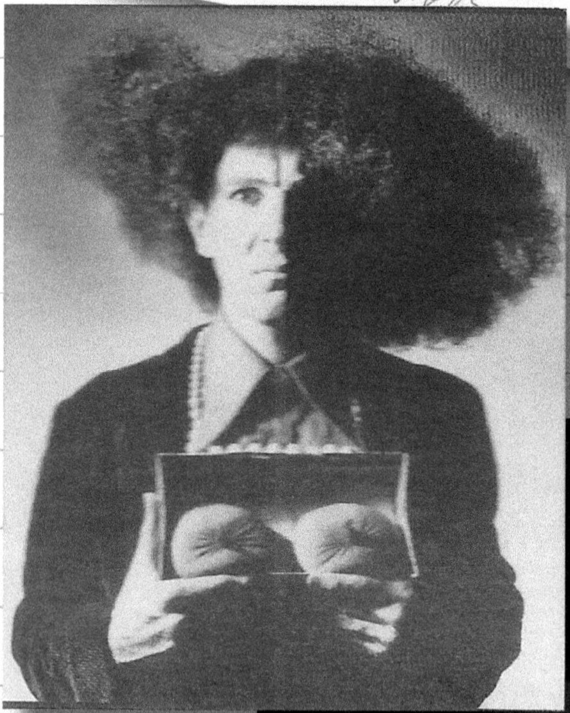

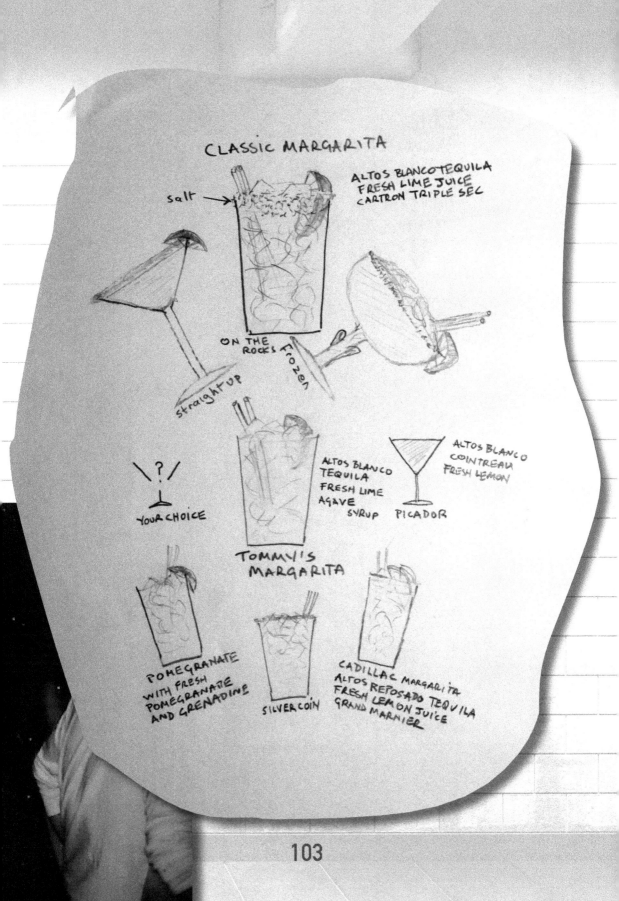

CLASSIC MARGARITA

salt →

ALTOS BLANCO TEQUILA
FRESH LIME JUICE
CARTRON TRIPLE SEC

ON THE ROCKS

Frozen

straight up

? YOUR CHOICE

ALTOS BLANCO
TEQUILA
FRESH LIME
AGAVE
SYRUP

TOMMY'S MARGARITA

ALTOS BLANCO
COINTREAU
FRESH LEMON

PICADOR

POMEGRANATE
WITH FRESH
POMEGRANATE
AND GRENADINE

SILVER COIN

CADILLAC MARGARITA
ALTOS REPOSADO TEQUILA
FRESH LEMON JUICE
GRAND MARNIER

MARQUEE

50MLS MAKERS
25MLS CHAMBORD
50MLS CRANBERRY

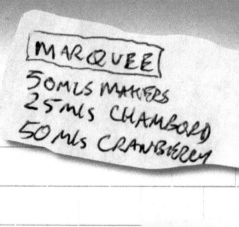

shake

NORTH SEA BREEZE

50mls BEEFEATER GIN
100mls GRAPEFRUIT
50mls LYCHEE JUICE

ICE
orange slice

SHAKE

PASSION FRUIT MOSITO

50mls CACHACA SAGATIBA
15mls passionfruit syrup
3 mint sprigs
25mls passionfruit puree
25mls lime juice
crushed ice

SHAKE

QUIET STORM

50 mls WYBOROWA vodka
15 mls lime juice
35 ml Lychee juice
35 ml pineapple.
35 ml guava juice
20 ml COCONUT CREAM
lime wedge
ice

SHAKE

RASPBERRY MULE

50 ml Wyborowa vodka
25 ml lime juice
5 raspberries
15 ml sugar syrup
ginger beer
crushed ice
lime wedge/raspberry

POUR

RUSSIAN BRIDE

35 mls STOLI VANILLA
10 mls WHITE CACAO
20 mls KAHLUA
50 mls cream (half + half)
ice
"Hundreds + thousands"

SHAKE

WHITE

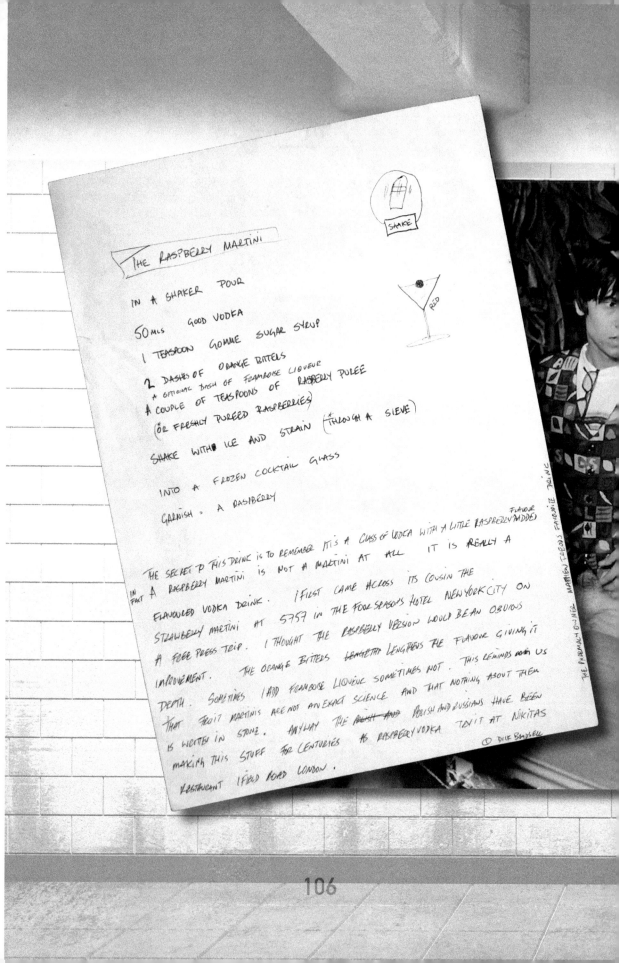

THE RASPBERRY MARTINI

IN A SHAKER POUR

50 MLS   GOOD VODKA

1 TEASPOON GOMME SUGAR SYRUP

2 DASHES OF ORANGE BITTERS
* OPTIONAL DASH OF FRAMBOISE LIQUEUR
A COUPLE OF TEASPOONS OF RASPBERRY PUREE
(OR FRESHLY PUREED RASPBERRIES)

SHAKE WITH ICE AND STRAIN (THROUGH A SIEVE)

INTO A FROZEN COCKTAIL GLASS

GARNISH = A RASPBERRY

THE SECRET TO THIS DRINK IS TO REMEMBER IT'S A GLASS OF VODKA WITH A LITTLE RASPBERRY FLAVOUR ADDED. IN FACT A RASPBERRY MARTINI IS NOT A MARTINI AT ALL   IT IS REALLY A FLAVOURED VODKA DRINK.   I FIRST CAME ACROSS ITS COUSIN THE STRAWBERRY MARTINI AT 5757 IN THE FOUR SEASONS HOTEL NEW YORK CITY ON A FREE PRESS TRIP.   I THOUGHT THE RASPBERRY VERSION WOULD BE AN OBVIOUS IMPROVEMENT.   THE ORANGE BITTERS LENGETHS LENGTHENS THE FLAVOUR GIVING IT DEPTH.   SOMETIMES I ADD FRAMBOISE LIQUEUR SOMETIMES NOT. THIS REMINDS US THAT FRUIT MARTINIS ARE NOT AN EXACT SCIENCE. AND THAT NOTHING ABOUT THEM IS WRITTEN IN STONE.   ANYWAY THE POLISH AND POLISH AND RUSSIANS HAVE BEEN MAKING THIS STUFF FOR CENTURIES AS RASPBERRY VODKA   TRY IT AT NIKITAS RESTAURANT 1 FIELD ROAD LONDON .

① DIVE BARDSELL

THE PARAMACH OWNER · MATTHEW FREUDS FAVOURITE DRINK

TATANKA

INTO A SHAKER FULL OF ICE POUR
50ml ZUBROWKA
150ml CLOUDY APPLE JUICE
SHAKE STRAIN OVER FRESH ICE
IN A TALL GLASS
NO GARNISH

TEQUILA OLD FASHIONED

15ml agave syrup
2 dashes orange bitters
50ml ALTOS REPO Tequila
ice
2 lemon twists

BUILD!

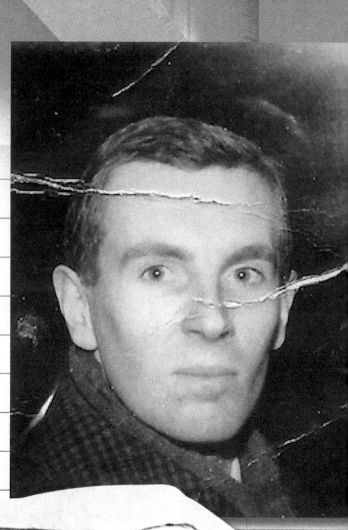

VANILLA DAIQUIRI

50ml Havana club
25ml lime juice
15ml vanilla syrup
ice
lime wedge

SHAKE

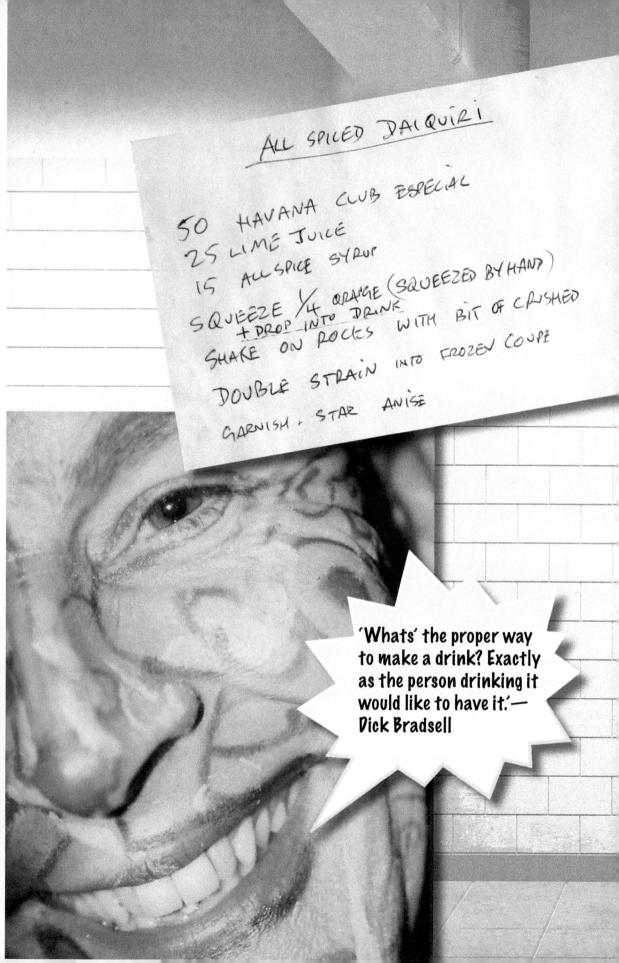

ORANGE/AMBER

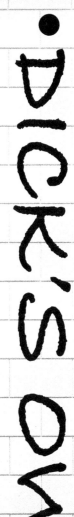

ALL-SPICED DAIQUIRI	MIXED BERRY JULEP
THE BRAMBLE	MORELLO CHERRY
CAROL CHANNING	COSMOPOLITIAN
CARSON MCCULLERS	ORANGE & ESPRESSO
CHILLI-PINA-RITA	MARTINI
DEVIL'S ADVOCAAT	PINK CHIHUAHUA
ESPRESSO MARTINI	PINK MOJITO
/ PHARMACEUTICAL	PLUM SOUR
STIMULANT / VODKA	POLISH MARTINI
ESPRESSO	POMEGRANATE & KAFFIR
GODDESS OF THE BRONX	FIZZ
GOLDEN RETRIEVER	ROSE PETAL MARTINI
HAVANA SUNRISE	RUM SHACK PUNCH
HEDGEROW SLING	RUSSIAN SPRING PUNCH
LADY BOY COCKTAIL	SNOW ON EARTH
LEMON MARTINI	STRAWBERRY MARTINEZ
THE LEMON COCKTAIL	SUMMER BREEZE
LAVENDER HONEY SOUR	THE THUNDERER
MANDARINE & PASSION	TIGER WOMAN
FRUIT MOJITO	THE TREACLE
MATCH SPRING PUNCH	THE WIBBLE

Want more recipes? Head to http://www.mixellany.com/dick-s-page.html or click the QR code. We'll be adding more to this list as we find them. Stay tuned.

Hello My name is Dick Bradsell and I'd like to tell you the story of how I invented The Bramble.

Many years ago 1986 I was working in The seminal young Persons wonders club in Carlisle St Soho called Fred's Club It was opened and owned by my old friend and colleague Fred Taylor and Adam Kidron (Baba Kidron then the film makers brother He and Fred were rich young chaps from West London and Freds dad was an architect.

and it AM The cool young people joined and it was quite a scene. Fred and I had met at the Zanzibar Club and Fred had gone on to manage the Groucho Club as assistant manager.

Fred's Club sold lots of good products including Breton cidre that the staff loved from a British french supplier called Cave Direct (I think) he owner supplied UK French restaurants. One day he brought in some a new to him products briottet liqueurs creme de Cassis framboise fraise and more par excellence I still stock them. We had two favourite gins original Bombay dry and High + Dry along with the house pours as soon as I sipped on this creme de mure I had my "Proustian" madelaine moment"

I was brought up in East Cowes Isle of Wight and spent my autumns + summers beating through the gorset bramble bushes of Ras Cowes Old Castle a run down ruin built by John Nash a 100 years before I ended up covered in scratches every day and semi dyed purple after harvesting these little jewels (as all bramble scrounges know use an ash stick and take the top fruit to avoid the fox and dog pee!

When I sipped the Briottet creme de mure I was right back on the chalk paths, amongst the brambles a juicey blackberry in my mouth How could I convert this memorable pleasure into a cocktail. A lovely British delectation It had to be a gin sour flavoured with more I decided traditional ratio trying it 8-2-1 or 6-2-1 seem to work. straight up it just didn't no delicacy Tooo cloying and over flavoured

So I remembered the Zanzibar and their gin sling Fall o'er crushed ice in a pilsner glass laced with Cherry flooring producing + wonderful "trickledown" effect a visual delight I took one of our double old fashioneds we made our Fred's version of the Mai Tai in and filled it with crushed ice

(a lovely trickle)

At Fred's Club invented The Bramble — A liqueur reminded me of my childhood, Blackberries in Autumn or Summer covered in purple! A British Drink.

SHAKE   OR BUILD

WHITLIME GREEN LACED WITH PURPLE

THE BRAMBLE

EITHER SHAKE
50 MLS GIN
25 MLS LEMON
2 BARSPOONS SUGAR SYRUP WITH ICE

AND POUR OVER CRUSHED ICE
IN LARGE WHISKY GLASS

[OR POUR ALL OVER CRUSHED ICE + STIR]
LACE WITH
ADD 20 MLS CRÈME DE MURE

GARNISH   BERRY + LEMON SLICE

MY 'MADELAINE' MOMENT

BLACKBERRY & LEMON SLICE

LOVELY & STRICKLE

BRAMBLE
GIN + FRESH LEMON + SUGAR
CREME DE MURE

Proust wrote about an involuntary memory of eating madeleines as a child in his novel In Search of Lost Time

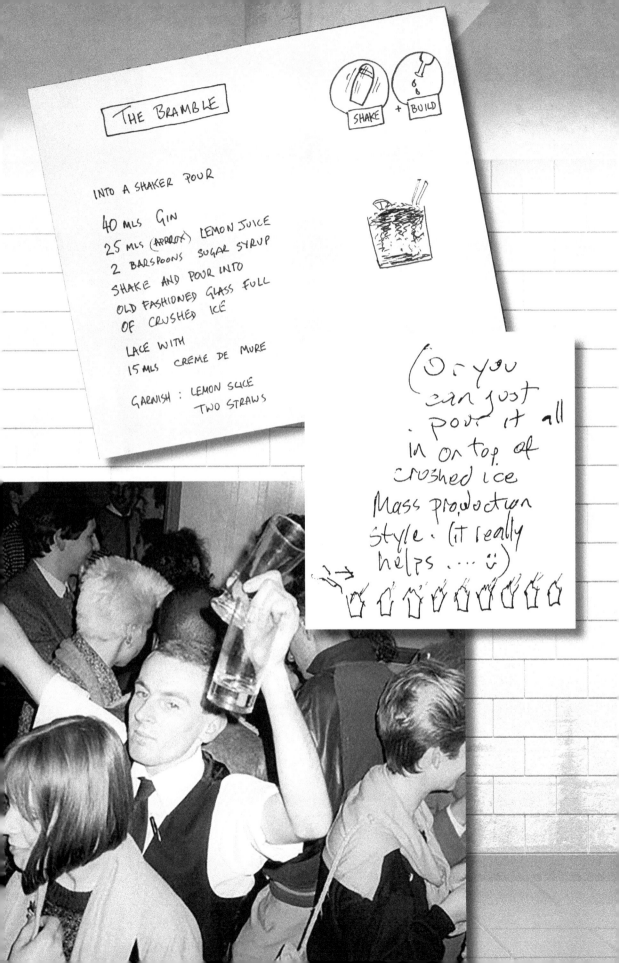

THE BRAMBLE

SHAKE + BUILD

INTO A SHAKER POUR

40 MLS GIN
25 MLS (APPROX) LEMON JUICE
2 BARSPOONS SUGAR SYRUP
SHAKE AND POUR INTO
OLD FASHIONED GLASS FULL
OF CRUSHED ICE

LACE WITH
15 MLS CREME DE MURE

GARNISH : LEMON SLICE
TWO STRAWS

(Or you can just pour it all in on top of crushed ice Mass production style. (it really helps .... ☺)

The Bramble.

I wanted to invent an English drink,
a British cocktail. So I used the
spirit, soured, sweetened and flavoured
template. Ratio being 50ml spirit;
25ml sour element; 12.5ml sweetner
(lessened to balance sweetness of
flavouring .. [The liqueur bit])

Gin, lemon juice, sugar and blackberry
liqueur as a straight up cocktail
doesn't quite work. So I used the
Zanzibar Singapore Sling recipe.
(50mls gin 25 mls lemon 10mls sugar syrup
over crushed ice in a tall (pilsner glass)
top with soda, lace with 15mls
cherry Heering, float of Benedictine
Orange/lemon/cherry "butterfly" two
straws)

Then some chap from a company brought
me Boutinot creme de mure from
France. First sip and I had "a" Madeleine
moment". It remined me of childhood

foraging for Blackberries in East Cowes Isle of Wight. In season we would be purple with scratches from trying to grasp wild blackberries from (above the dags + foxes piss line) on the Bramble bushes on the land of Old East Cowes Castle.

So I made this: (with Spanish lemons, french mure + bombay dry gin)

The Bramble

In shaker base glass
50mls good gin
25 mls fresh lemon
10mls (...hmm) sugar syrup
Shake with ice. Strain
into double old fashioned
(or old fashioned) full of crushed
ice. Add little more crushed ice.
two sipper straws +
blackberry (or raspberry
if you haven't got any)
lace with 12.5 mls
Creme de mure
add lemon slice

(a lovely trickle)

(Or you can just pour it all in on top of crushed ice Mass production style. (it really helps .... ☺)

→ ▽▽▽▽▽▽▽▽▽

[It's gin lemon sugar blackberry liqueur... got it!?]

CARA CHANNING

150ml* champagne (depends* glass size (or is it 100 or 125)

15ml FRAMBOISE EAU DE VIE
10 ml FRAMBOISE LIQUEUR
5 ml sugar syrup

garnish: a raspberry

POUR

light pink 'oil in water'

champ flute

CARSON McCULLER

IN A CHAMPAGNE GLASS
15MLS GINGER + LEMON GRASS SYRUP
25 ML CHILLED VODKA
TOP WITH CHAMPAGNE

Devil's Advocaat

Advocaat 25
coriel 25
chambord 25
2sp vanilla sugar
3 fresh raspberies
Dash lime
Dash lemonade

CHILLI - PINA - RITA

(CHILLIPINARITA)

350 mls Tequila

in shaker steel 25 mls lime
12.5 mls Triplesec   +

shake together with ice
pour over ice int Tumbler
1 slice pineapple   2 slices chilli (red)

muddle in shaker glass
3 slices of red chilli
3 wedges pineapple
10 ml's pineapple syrup

(shake / muddle)

FROZEN CHILLI-
PINARITA

AND BIG STRAWS

3 pieces pineapple
2 pieces chilli
Dash chilli sauce
25 lime
35 HOUSE
oz TEQUILA
50
12.5 ml PINEAPPLE
SYRUP
25 ml Pineapple juice
Blended

Pineapple stick/wedge
dipped in squeezed lime
then "chilli salt"
glass rimmed with chilli salt

RIM GLASS
CHILLI
+ SALT
STUFF
PINEAPPLE
WEDGE
(COATED
IN LIME
+ CHILLI
SALT STUFF

So one Chilli-Pina-Rita is
frozen and the other is a natural just like Daiquiris come in
frappeéd and natural versions.
Up to the customer's taste,
really.

<u>The Espresso Martini</u>
<u>The Vodka Espresso</u>
<u>The Pharmaceutical Stimulant</u>

Being conclusive can, at sometimes, be somewhat difficult.

There I was working away in the busy Soho Brasserie. Coffee grounds leaking into my ice well when a young woman asked "Give me a drink that will wake me up then fuck me up". Who was she? I have no idea. I was told "An American model" by a friend Keir McCloud. I truely don't know but that was the inspiration for this drink

<u>The Vodka Espresso:</u>

50 mls good vodka
12.5 mls Kahlua
a dash of sugar
a shot of <u>extra</u> extra strong espresso coffee
Shake on ice. Pour all over rocks in a small old fashioned glass two sipper straws (optional)

← white foam
← black

SHAKE

Later at Match EC1 a chap called Vasco and I made the straight up "martini version"

50 ml vodka
12.5 ml Kahlua
10 ml Tia Maria
5 ml sugar syrup
<u>extra</u> extra strong espresso
shake strain prechilled glass
3 coffee beans (for luck) garnish

← white foam
← black

the beans

At the Pharmacy Damian Hirst renamed it. <u>It is the same recipe</u>
The Pharmacuetical Stimulant
So that's that!

25/5/2015

Doubt + confusion?
I was there.

Not with me

Espresso Martini at Match
first at Soho Brasserie
   then Match [Portuguese Sea Captain]

Then Pharmacy

Ooh the
Controversy
(that is cocktails)

ESPRESSO MARTINI

INTO A SHAKER FULL OF ICE POUR

35 MLS VODKA

BARSPOON   SUGAR SYRUP
   "   KAHLUA
   "   TIA MARIA

FINALLY   A SERVING OF (HOT
OR COLD) FRESH ESPRESSO

SHAKE
STRAIN INTO PRE CHILLED COCKTAIL
GLASS

GARNISH: 3 coffee BEANS

SHAKE

DIFFERENT WAYS
WITH 3 COFFEEBEANS

ESPRESSO MARTINI
VODKA + KAHLUA + TIA MARIA
VERY STRONG ESPRESSO + SUGAR

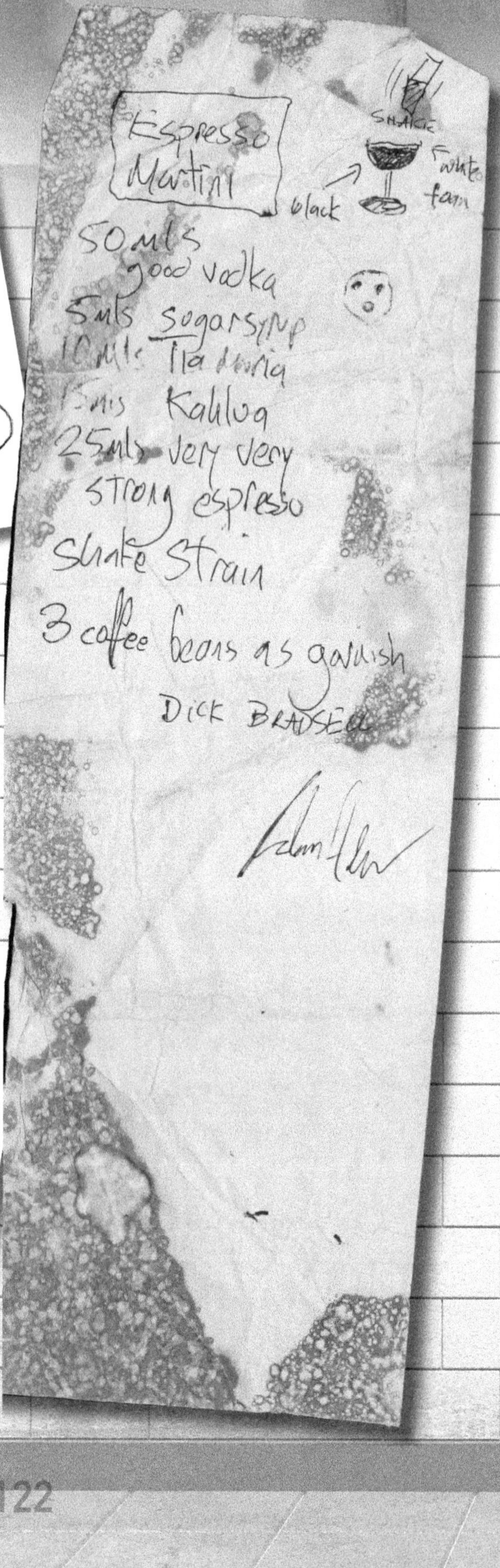

Espresso Martini

SHAKE → black → white foam

50 mls good vodka
5 mls sugar syrup
10 mls Tia Maria
5 mls Kahlua
25 mls very very strong espresso
Shake Strain

3 coffee beans as garnish

DICK BRADSELL

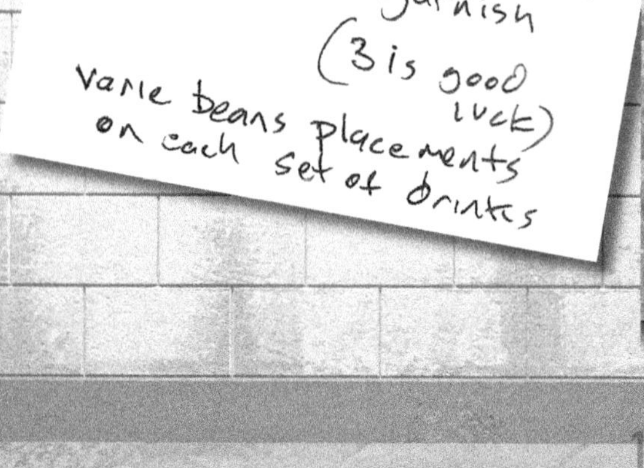

← white foam
black!
← 3 coffee bean garnish
(3 is good luck)
Varie beans placements on each set of drinks

Espresso Martini / Pharmaceutal Stimulant

Into empty shaker glass
50mls good vodka
5mls cane sugar syrup

5mls Tia Maria
10mls Kahlua
25mls double strength espresso (and the better the coffee the better the drink!) Add ice, shake, strain into prechilled cocktail glass
3 coffee beans as garnish (and if you can see through it or it is brown not black its wrong)

the beans → white foam

black

the beans

123

Espresso Martini

I used to work in this place called the Soho Brasserie on Old Compton St Soho. It was about 1980 something We made a lot of coffees and it was a Sue Miles led proper copy of a French Brasserie and old Soho hated it cos it was shoved in the Helvitia pub {a filthy scum hole} It was quite good, very tosy and everyone I knew drank there. It was trendy (the Gray Organisation, Absolute Begginers)

I had coffee grouts leaking into my ice well when some young lady ... who? asked for a drink — a cocktail — she was American? "what would you like" "Something that's gonna wake me up, then fuck me up" Huge grin Then I came up with

50mls vodka
5mls sugar syrup
15mls Kahlua
shot of very strong espresso
Shaken strained over
rocks. No garnish

VODKA ESPRESSO

← whitefoam

← black

small old fashioned

I called it the Vodka Espresso

Then I was working at Match, the first one
Clerkenwell Road
And it was cocktail becoming Martinis
and all cocktails were a xxxxxx Martini
{USA rediscovering The cocktail hour?}
I'd been to NYC on an Absolut trip with
John Beech and he'd taken me to
50/50 at the Four Seasons   Where they had
an Absolut promotion on cocktail shaker
full of five "flavoured" "Martini"s
I worked with a guy called Vasco {Portuguese sea-
captain} he was great. He made the Vodka
Espresso as a Martini - Espresso Martini!
It needed adjustment. I used the ratio pineapple
behind the Brandy Alexander as a template
~~xxxxx~~ (espresso to vodka with 3 flavours
in between) and it became

Espresso martini
30mls vodka
5mls sugar syrup
5mls Tia Maria
10 mls Kahlua
a short 25mls of
very very strong
  espresso shaken
strained pre chilled cocktail glass

white foam
black!
← 3
coffee bean
garnish
(3 is good
luck)
varie beans placements
on each set of drinks

So I guess Vasco + I invented it.
(Where art thou --- wanderer?)

Then I had to go work at The DNA
bar Quo Vadis to find out why it was
so horrid. Damian Hirst hated the place
and he had invested / given his art + soul
to it and he didn't like going there
(or his friends did not...?)

So he got me to do The Pharmacy
I had to invent 20 drinks = recipe
for 20 shit drinks. So I got given
names by Damian and ~~poet~~ drink
recipes to those names (and invented a
few ... The Formalin Martini is pretty good).

Thus The Pharmicotical Stimulant
is Damian Hirst's name for the
previous Espresso Martini recipe
(and it wasn't Kate Moss [who ~~gets~~ looks
younger as she gets older --- good trick luv])

That's it

Espresso Martini / Pharmcutal Stimulant

Into empty shaker glass
50 mls   good vodka
5 mls cane sugar syrup

5 mls   Tia Maria
10 mls   Kahlua
25 mls   double strength
espresso (and the better
the coffee the better
the drink!) Add ice,
shake, strain into
prechilled cocktail glass
3 coffee beans as Garnish
(and if you can see through it
or it is brown not black
its wrong)

Some young lady from Australasia was in Pink Chi-
wahua recently asked if she could tell me
how to make it "her way." When I got over
myself I realised it was pretty good recipe
50 vodka 25 kahlua shot of very strong
espresso. Yum... A robust recipe can
take a few variations (the Cosmo!?)
Any way I've see most of them via the

opening of Manchester's Living Room
(by the much underrated Paul Newman)
They did every variant Baileys, Frangelico
Contreau etc etc   just after Match
Ecl. (I've only ever drunk one whole
espresso Martini . It kinda fuck's you
up. I really don't need to talk any more
than I do already....)

(At the NY/London Absolut return
thingy we did recently. the helpful young
folk (are they interns? pay the workers! its
a goddam job ... you get money for work!)
Made the coffee so concentrated and strong
Nick S. had to water it down and (still
was getting a contact high!) Moderation ...
These espresso + alcohol things are
dangerous (oh yeah ... that's why I invented
it.... ☺)

"What would you like" "Something
that's gonna wake me up, then fuck me up"
Huge grin Then I came up with

50mls vodka
5mls sugar syrup
15mls Kahlua
shot of very strong espresso
Shaken strained over
rocks. No garnish

VODKA ESPRESSO

← whitefoam

black

small
oldfashioned

I called it the Vodka Espresso

ESPRESSO

VODKA ESPRESSO

whitefoam

black

small
oldfashioned

50mls vodka
5mls sugar syrup
15mls Kahlua
shot of very strong espresso
Shaken strained over
rocks. No garnish
I called it the Vodka Espresso

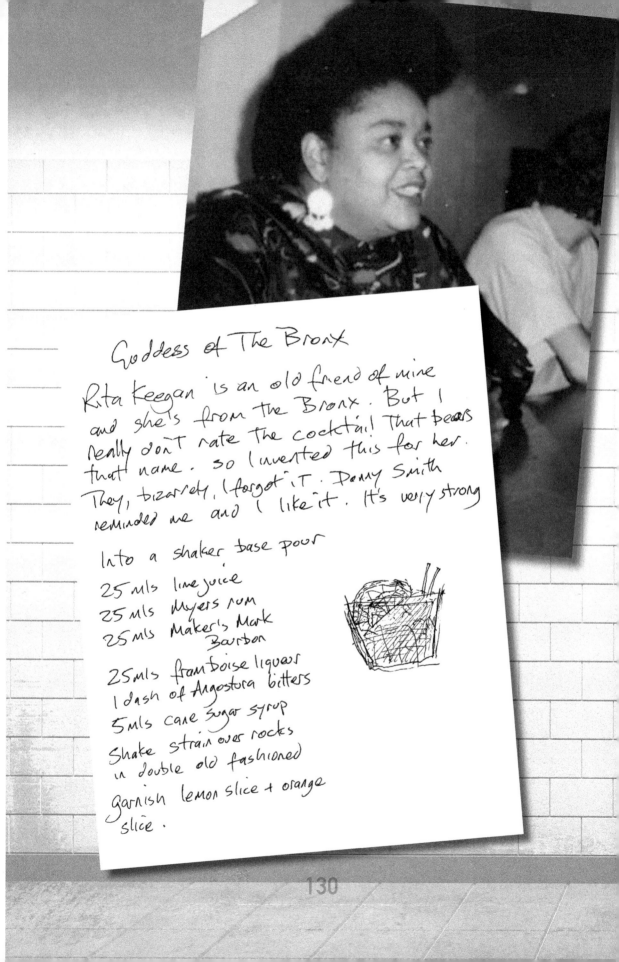

Goddess of The Bronx

Rita Keegan is an old friend of mine and she's from the Bronx. But I really don't rate the cocktail That bears that name. So I invented this for her. They, bizarrely, I forgot it. Danny Smith reminded me and I like it. It's very strong

Into a shaker base pour

25 mls lime juice
25 mls Myers rum
25 mls Maker's Mark Bourbon

25 mls framboise liquor
1 dash of Angostura bitters
5 mls cane sugar syrup
Shake strain over rocks
in double old fashioned
Garnish lemon slice + orange slice.

ORANGE TWIST

GOLDEN RETRIEVER

HAVANA 3YO RUM
GREEN CHARTREUSE
DARK CACAO LIQUER

AFTER 3 OF THESE,
YOU'll NEED 1 OF THESE

HAVANA SUNRISE

INTO A "DANGEROUS" GLASS POUR

25 ML	HAVANA RUM 3 y'OLD
100 ML	PINEAPPLE JUICE
100 ML	ORANGE JUICE
15 ML THEN	GRENADINE

SQUEEZE + DROP IN TWO WEDGES OF LIME INTO DRINK

TOP WITH 25 ML HAVANA 3 y'OLD RUM

A "dangerous glass" is a tall, skinny, tippy pilsner glass...really popular in bars for while until one too many drinks tipped over.

HEDGEROW SLING

SHAKE + BUILD

INTO A SHAKER FULL OF ICE

POUR

JUICE OF A LEMON (40MLS)
15MLS SUGAR SYRUP
35MLS SLOE GIN

SHAKE
STRAIN OVER ROCKS IN TALL GLASS

TOP NEARLY WITH SODA

ADD CRUSHED ICE

LACE WITH 20MLS
CREME DE MURE

GARNISH: LIME WEDGE

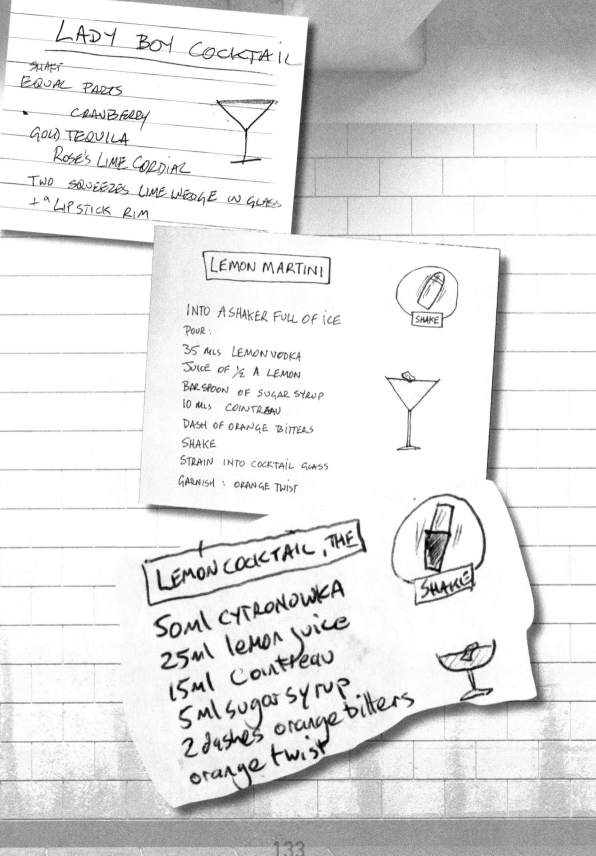

LADY BOY COCKTAIL

SHAKE
EQUAL PARTS

- CRANBERRY
- GOLD TEQUILA
- ROSE'S LIME CORDIAL

TWO SQUEEZES LIME WEDGE IN GLASS
+ A LIPSTICK RIM

LEMON MARTINI

INTO A SHAKER FULL OF ICE
POUR:

35 MLS LEMON VODKA
JUICE OF ½ A LEMON
BARSPOON OF SUGAR SYRUP
10 MLS COINTREAU
DASH OF ORANGE BITTERS
SHAKE
STRAIN INTO COCKTAIL GLASS
GARNISH : ORANGE TWIST

SHAKE

LEMON COCKTAIL, THE

SHAKE

50ml CYTRONOWKA
25ml lemon juice
15ml Cointreau
5ml sugar syrup
2 dashes orange bitters
orange twist

LAVENDER HONEY SOUR

35   JAMESON

25   LEMON JUICE

15   BENEDICTINE

15   LAVENDER HONEY MIX

25 mls EGG WHITE

1 DASH PEYCHAUD BITTERS

SHAKE   DOUBLE STRAIN
INTO 'SOUR STEM' GLASS
GARNISH   ROSE BUD

← AMBER

MANDARINE + PASSION FRUIT MOJITO

10 MINT LEAVES RUB IN HANDS RUBBED AROUND RIM

50 ML HAVANA

20 mls MANDARIN PUREE

~~10 MINT LEAVES~~

7.5 mls LIME JUICE

15 ML PASSION FRUIT SYRUP

1 SCOOP CRUSHED

CHURN 10 SECONDS

TOP CRUSHED

GARNISH MINT SPRIG

HOW I INVENT DRINKS

NEW PRODUCT : A NEW PRODUCT COMES ON THE MARKET
OR AVAILABLE — WE EXPERIMENT AND COME UP WITH A NEW DRINK
                LYCHEE + ROSE PETAL MARTINI
                CARAMEL MANHATTAN

                A BRAMBLE — MULE DRINK

NAME   HONEY WALL
OR CONCEIT

                                        SUMMER BREEZE

TWIST
ON A CLASSIC

PONT BERRY MARTIN

THE
1) THUNDERER   TIMES OFFICIAL
                    COCKTAIL
2) BRAMBLE

SNOW ON EARTH   SNOOD
                    MURDEKIN
RUSSIAN SPRING PUNCH

BIKINI MARTINI

WIBBLE

DETROIT MARTINI

RASPBERRY MARTINI
POLISH MARTINI
3) ESPRESSO MARTINI / VODKA
                    ESPRESSO
CAROL CHANNING

PLUM SOUR

CORAL FIZZ

ROSE PETAL MARTINI

GOLDEN RETRIEVER

GIN + ELDERFLOWER SOUR

THE
LEMON
COCKTAIL
(LEMON
MARTINI)

Dear Michael,

I am sorry Candy has caused a problem about the Russian Spring Punch the dispute about its content has been the bane of my life for a very long time. Just ask Sly, Jennifer, Johnathan Downey or any one else I have trained or worked recently with. I am adamant that the drink is far better without the inclusion of raspberry puree. This makes the drink imbalanced and unsubtle - unfortunately as the "Match Spring Punch" at Match it is our biggest selling drink by far so the bottle is lost there.

When I invented it for a party in 1982 it was based on a true punch (like a Planters Punch) and the balance in the drink comes from those ratios

PTO

This letter confirms
the birth of the
Match Spring Punch.

TALL GLASS OF ICE
50 mls VODKA
25 mls LEMON JUICE
3 teaspoons sugar syrup
3 teaspoons cassis

stirred and topped with champagne
lemon slice , berries etc

You can imagine how pissed off I was to return to Match EC1 last year and find that they were slopping loads of red puree in my masterpiece!

Thank you for keeping the faith. I appreciate it greatly.

I write this as I happen to be writing my latest rant for CLASS MAG about people messing with drinks other people have created. That is a prime example. Grrrr!

Dick A. Bradsell

MIXED BERRY JULEP

2 MINT SPRIGS (RUB IN HAND)
RUB AROUND RIM OF TIN
80mls MIXED BERRY PUREE
25 FOUR ROSES
25 MARTELL
5 mls DEMARA SUGAR MIX
1 SCOOP CRUSHED
CHURN 10 SECS
ADD MORE CRUSHED

IN A TIN

THEN DRIZZLE 5mls MORE

GARNISH FROZEN BLACKBERRY + MINT

MORELLO CHERRY COSMOPOLITAN

40 mls   ABSOLUT CITRON
             COINTREAU
20   CRANBERRY + MORELLO MIX
25
10 LIME
DASH ORANGE BITTERS

SHAKE
DOUBLE STRAIN INTO FROZEN COUPE
FLAMED ORANGE ZEST + DISCARD
GARNISH   A   GRIOLETTE CHERRY

CHERRY RED

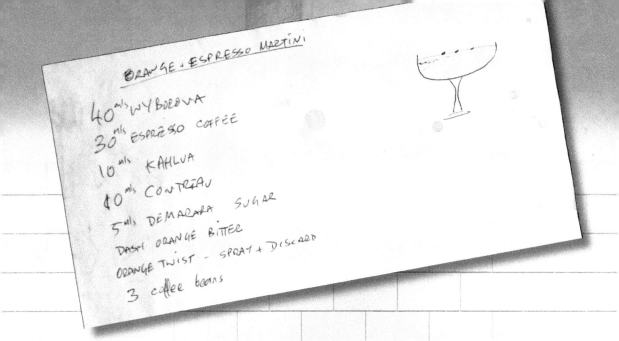

ORANGE + ESPRESSO MARTINI

40 mls WYBOROWA
30 mls ESPRESSO COFFEE
10 mls KAHLUA
10 mls CONTREAU
5 mls DEMARARA SUGAR
DASH ORANGE BITTER
ORANGE TWIST - SPRAY + DISCARD
3 coffee beans

PINK MOJITO

50mls ALTOS TEQUILA
25mls LIME JUICE
3 sprigs of Mint
100mls cranberry juice
crushed ice

SHAKE

PLUM SOUR

pink

25mls Chinese Plum wine
25mls Scotch J+B
25mls lemon juice
10mls sugar syrup
10mls egg white
Peychaud bitters
lemon wheel/cherry

SHAKE

POMEGRANATE + KAFFIR FIZZ

CHILL HI BALL GLASS

50 mls	PLYMOUTH
25 mls	POMEGRANATE JUICE
20 mls	LIME JUICE
15 mls	KAFFIR LIME SYRUP LEAF
20 mls	EGG WHITE

DOUBLE STRAIN

SHAKE
FOR 5 SECS
HARD

TOP WITH SODA
CANAL ZEST LIME STRINGS - WHACK MINT GARNISH

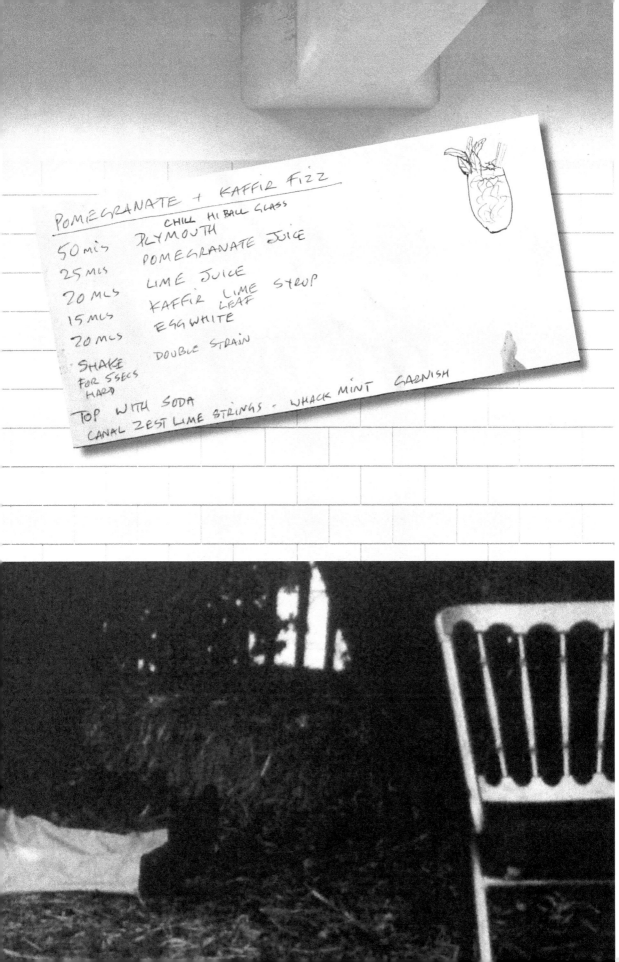

The Rose Petal Martini.

If I come across new products or discover a use for an old unusual one I am very pleased. Inspiration. (tried mixing Lanique Rose petal vodka liqueur with Rubicon lychee juice (when it came to my local shop) I tried the ratio 1:1:1. 3 equal parts, with Bombay Sapphire gin. And it just worked. Peychaud bitters improved it. It is very sweet but people like a sweet drink sometimes and I really like it. Make sure the petal is edible. Some flowers are poisonous! A poison garnish is a bit Agatha Christie. I teach people to try it shaken, to see why it should be stirred. Far complex when stirred. One flavour when shaken. I know there are other versions of this drink and this is not the first rose petal martini. But I won a competition with it .. so fuck off!

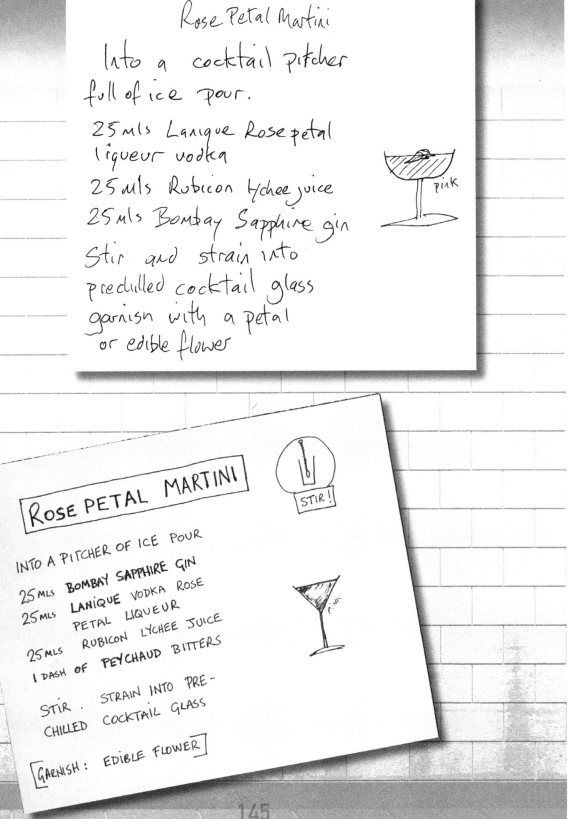

Rose Petal Martini

Into a cocktail pitcher
full of ice pour.

25 mls Lanique Rose petal
liqueur vodka
25 mls Rubicon lychee juice
25 mls Bombay Sapphire gin

Stir and strain into
prechilled cocktail glass
garnish with a petal
or edible flower

pink

ROSE PETAL MARTINI

STIR!

INTO A PITCHER OF ICE POUR

25 MLS BOMBAY SAPPHIRE GIN
25 MLS LANIQUE VODKA ROSE
PETAL LIQUEUR
25 MLS RUBICON LYCHEE JUICE
1 DASH OF PEYCHAUD BITTERS

STIR. STRAIN INTO PRE-
CHILLED COCKTAIL GLASS

GARNISH: EDIBLE FLOWER

PINK

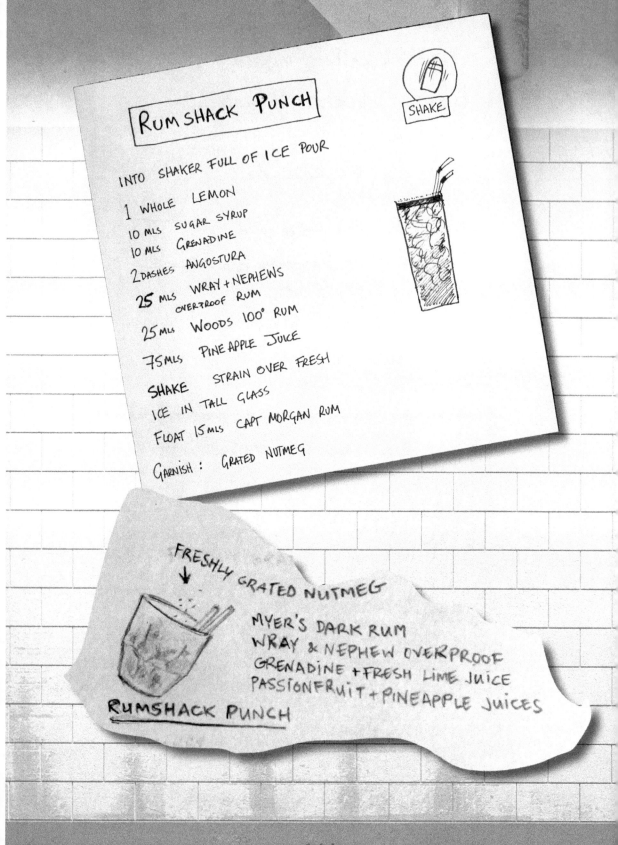

RUMSHACK PUNCH

INTO SHAKER FULL OF ICE POUR

1 WHOLE LEMON
10 MLS SUGAR SYRUP
10 MLS GRENADINE
2 DASHES ANGOSTURA
25 MLS WRAY + NEPHEWS OVERPROOF RUM
25 MLS WOODS 100° RUM
75 MLS PINEAPPLE JUICE
SHAKE STRAIN OVER FRESH ICE IN TALL GLASS
FLOAT 15 MLS CAPT MORGAN RUM

GARNISH: GRATED NUTMEG

SHAKE

FRESHLY GRATED NUTMEG
↓

MYER'S DARK RUM
WRAY & NEPHEW OVERPROOF
GRENADINE + FRESH LIME JUICE
PASSIONFRUIT + PINEAPPLE JUICES

RUMSHACK PUNCH

Russian Spring Punch

Years ago when I was a naughty elf and played in the land of London. I was asked to make cocktails for Peter and Rebecca Dupont de Bie's Party at their house in Kensington? (poz, still get lost around there. Posh people land). I suggested they got everyone to bring a bottle of fizz (champagne, prossecco± or muck?)

I made glasses (plastic cups) full of ice and a mix of Vodka, lemon and cassis. You just topped it up with fizz and drant through a straw. It was quite a wild party. Several divorces, various falls on the stairs car accidents. I took the drink and made it at Fred's Club. Shake the vodka lemon + cassis + sugar. Strain into tall glass over ice + top with champagne. It would fizz up + take ages until a young sensible person told me to "quell" the champ with the vodka. I hadn't thought of that ... 5 years jeez ...!

148

Russian Spring Punch

Into shaker

25mls lemon juice
10 mls sugar syrup
15mls cassis

Shake with ice
Pour over rocks
in tall glass
(very tall glass)

top with champagne
and vodka (at same time
to prevent champagne bubbling
up over glass... ie Quelling)

You can use old (yesterdays) champagne
but it should be dry + taste of the
champagne when the drink is made
(But people like it sweeter
and it is lethal so let them
have what they like but please
don't add puree)

garnish is a lemon slice
and raspberry but a
sprig of currants? blackcurrents
is a visual treat .... ☺

(You can bang these out pretty fast if you make
a lemon sugar cassis mix. Then pour the vodka
and champagne over it in the glass of ice)

Pink

Russian Spring Punch
Gin g fizz add to glass of vodka
cassis
+lemon juice

a wild party for Peter Kent RIP
+ Rebecca Du pont de Bie
lethal

RUSSIAN SPRING PUNCH

POUR

INTO A LARGE COUPE GLASS

POUR
7 CUBES OF ICE
JUICE OF 1 LEMON
10 mls SUGAR SYRUP
10 mls CASSIS

TOP WITH CHAMPAGNE
WHILST QUELLING WITH
15 mls VODKA

GARNISH: LEMON SLICE

PINK

RUSSIAN SPRING PUNCH

← PINK!

VODKA
CASSIS
LEMON
SUGAR
CHAMPAGNE

Wish Dick had put the measures on this shooter. (Probably equal parts with cream on the top.)

SNOW ON EARTH

KAHLUA + CHAMBORD + CREAM

STRAWBERRY MARTINEZ
2 SPOONS STRAWBERRY JAM
50ML BEEFEATER GIN
10 MLS DUBONNET
DASH MARISCHINO
DASH ORANGE ~~FLOWER WATER~~ BITTERS
20MLS EGG WHITE
SHAKE ON ROCKS
DOUBLE STRAIN INTO FROZEN COUPE
GARNISH FROZEN STRAWBERRY SLICE

SUMMER BREEZE
50ml WYBOROWA VODKA
100ml cranberry juice
15ml elderflower syrup
50ml pressed apple juice
ice
orange slice

SHAKE

pink

151

The Thunderer

I was asked to compete with a few people to create a cocktail of the martini style for The Times Newspaper (when it was The Thunderer...) by Jane McQuItty. I worked on it with Richard Crack at the Zanzibar. We thought of the Rikky Dikkytini. It was orginally made with Stolychana but they didn't like the russian connection so I used Wyborowa from Poland (communist Poland...?!) and stated my love affair with polish products. A customer, barrister Andrew Colman (well he is a friend now) persuaded me to try it with Zubrowka. He's right it is better

Into a Stirring Pitcher full of ice

The Thunderer

50mls Wyborowa chilled (or Zubrowka)

1 bar spoon of Parfait amour

3 drops of cassis
stir strain pre chilled glass
No garnish
And do use very cold vodka
(a lemon twist or a berry is nice

← lilac colour

← very cold glass

Went to Soho brasserie + worked in Chain bars + pub bars
Changing old Soho

Into a Stirring Pitcher full of ice

The Thunderer

50mls Wyborowa
chilled (or Zubrowka)

1 bar spoon of
Parfait amour

3 drops of cassis
stir strain pre chilled
No garnish   glass
And do use very cold vodka
(a lemon twist or a berry is nice

← lilac colour
← very cold glass

THUNDERER, THE

50ml Wyborowa
        Vodka   STIR

3 drops cassis
5 ml Parfait amour
lemon twist
ice

THE THUNDERER

STIR

IN A PITCHER FULL OF ICE POUR

75mls POLISH VODKA (ie not Russian) FROZEN

A DASH OR TWO OF CASSIS
2 TEASPOONS PARFAIT AMOUR

STIR THOROUGHLY

STRAIN INTO PRE CHILLED
MARTINI GLASS

NO GARNISH

PALE
VIOLET

THIS IS THE FIRST DRINK I EVER INVENTED. IT WAS AT THE ZANZIBAR CLUB IN THE VERY EARLY 80's. THERE WAS A COCKTAIL COMP FOR THE OFFICIAL TIMES COCKTAIL AND THIS ONE. IT HAD TO BE A MARTINI AND HAD TO BE PURPLE AS I RECALL. ANOTHER (AGING) BARTENDER RICHARD HELPED ME WITH IT BUT IT IS MOSTLY MY OWN WORK. EVEN TODAY IT IS THE OFFICIAL TIMES COCKTAIL. I ORIGINALLY MADE IT WITH STOLYCHNIA + STIPULATED THIS DUE TO ITS QUALITY BUT BECAUSE OF THE POLITICAL SITUATION AT THE TIME THEY ASKED IF I COULD CHANGE THE NATIONALITY OF THE MAIN INGREDIENT. THAT SLIGHTLY PUT MY NOSE OUT OF JOINT SO I TESTED THEIR POLITICS BY THEN STIPULATING THAT EXCELLENT EXAMPLE BRAND OF POLISH VODKA WYBOROWA THIS PASSED MUSTER AND STARTED MY RELATIONSHIP WITH THE VODKAS OF POLAND AND THE COUNTRY ITSELF.

There's a typo in this recipe. This 'one' DID win!

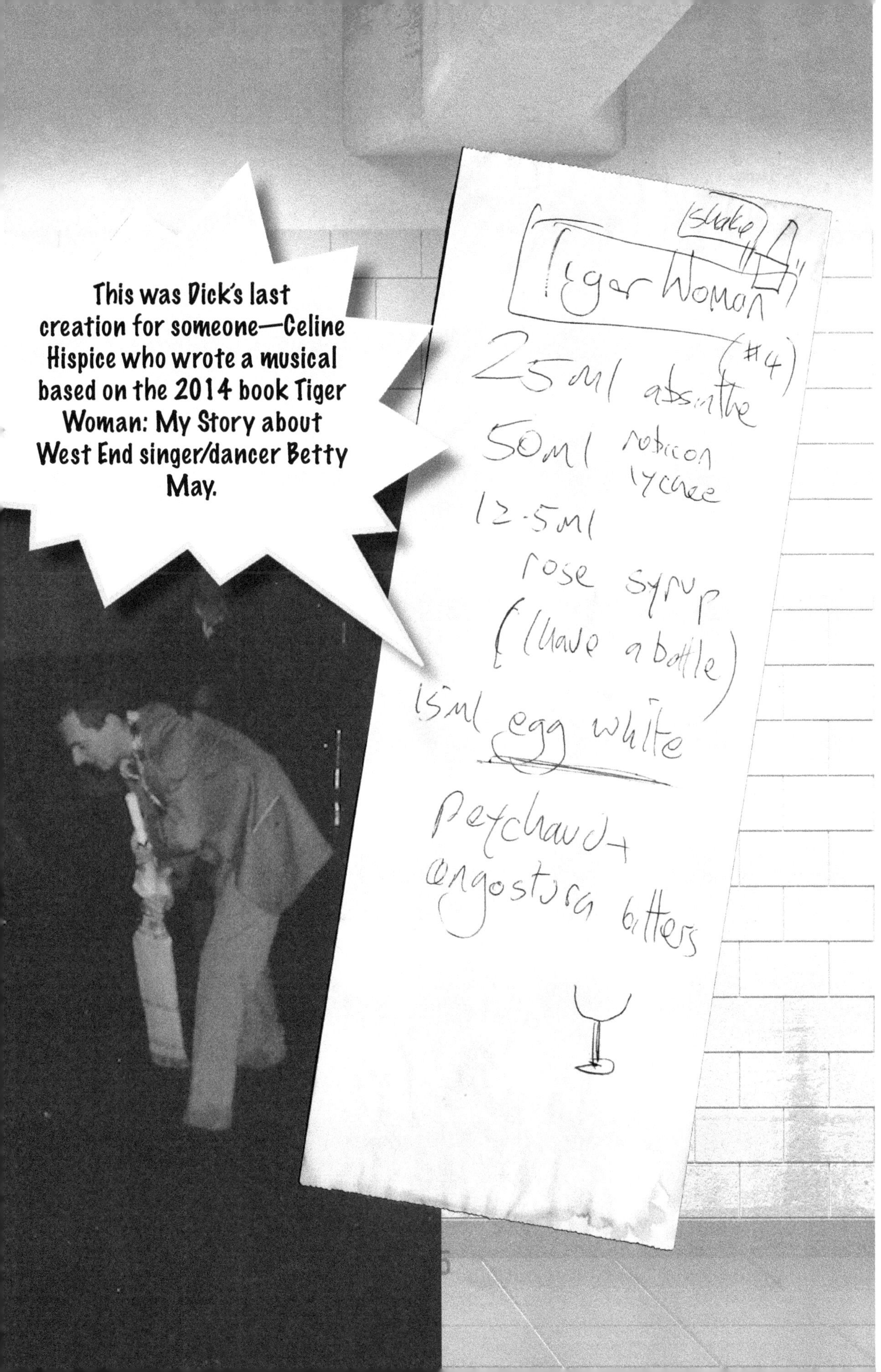

This was Dick's last creation for someone—Celine Hispice who wrote a musical based on the 2014 book Tiger Woman: My Story about West End singer/dancer Betty May.

Tiger Woman (#4) "shake"

25ml absinthe

50ml robicon lychee

12.5ml rose syrup
(I have a bottle)

15ml egg white

Petchaud + angostura bitters

The Treacle

I heard the story of the british apple
farming industry's demise. And
now they make concentrated/carton
apple juice. The clear stuff.
And I really like rum and myers is
much underrated. It's great in cocktails.

Make like an old fashioned (its an
old fashioned made with little sugar myers
rum and a splash of apple juice with a
lemon twist)

Into an old fashioned glass
1 teaspoon cane sugar syrup
2 dashes of Angostura
stir with 1 cube of ice
add 25mls Myers rum
1 cube ice and stir
and two cubes ice stir
25mls Myers and stir
1 ice cube stir
20mls concentrated apple juice
(the cheap clear stuff)
Garnish a lemon twist (or two)

It should
taste like
treacle....?

156

The Wibble   Nick Blacknell (Plymouth Sloe Gin) Detroit Bar
on the spot

WIBBLE, THE

SHAKE

25ml sloe gin
25ml Beefeater gin
25ml Grapefruit juice
5ml Mure
5ml sugar syrup
5ml lemon juice
lemon twist
ice

LEMON TWIST

THE WIBBLE

SLOE GIN + GIN + CREME DE MURE
GRAPEFRUIT JUICE
FRESH LEMON JUICE
SUGAR

MAKES YOU
WOBBLE BUT
NOT FALL OVER

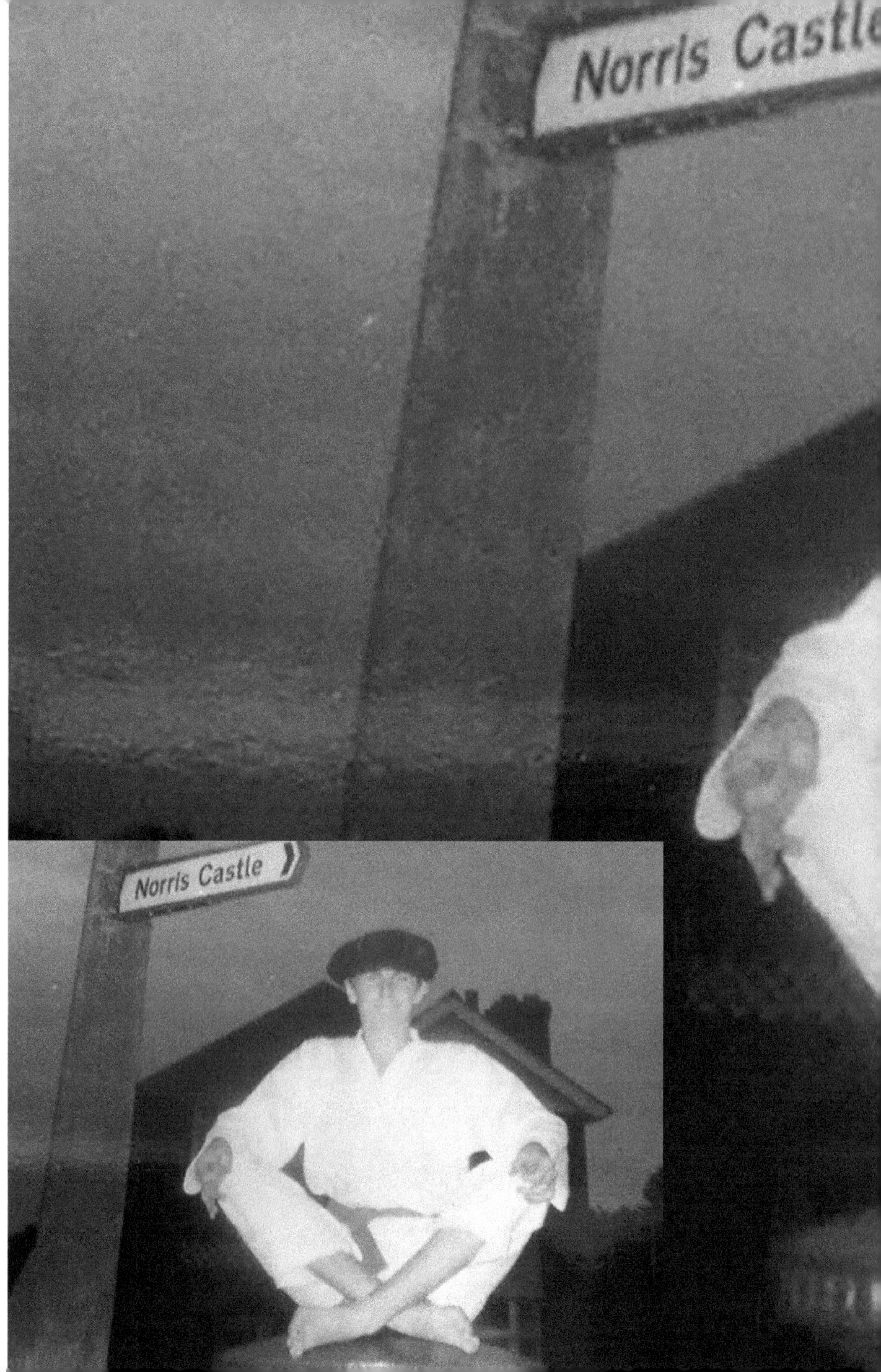
Norris Castle

DICK'S

COCKTAIL

COURSE

Dick put together
this training course back in 2003.
While some bartending methods and
techniques have changed, most of
what is in this chapter is still very
relevant today. A few tips and hand-
written thoughts appear, too.

FOR BEGINNERS

We are going to teach you the basic skills you need to work behind a cocktail bar.
—How to shake, stir, muddle and blend, layer and build.
—How to be clean, speedy and efficient
—How to read a recipe
—How to read an order
—How to make some basic cocktails (Tom Collins, Planters Punch, Margarita, Tequila Sunrise, Cosmopolitan, Sea Breeze, Maritni & B52)

1. Set Up

Here is a bar set up...
1. Bar set-ups have been around a long time. A bar in 1926, 1959 and 1993 would all look very similar.
2. There are many ways to set up a bar.
3. Cocktail bartending has different needs, so the bar will be set up differently to a pub or wine bar to cater for these needs. It is like a kitchen, it is about:
   - Efficiency
   - Economics
   - Common sense
   - The drinks need to be made quickly, well and with style.
4. Cocktail bartenders are always on display—this is a vital part of their job.
5. Everything you require must be available at the bar.
6. Someone else will need to use the bar space too. The way you work has a direct impact on others.

You may have a starting/finishing procedures list for your bar which tells you what to do to prepare/set up; you should learn and follow this.

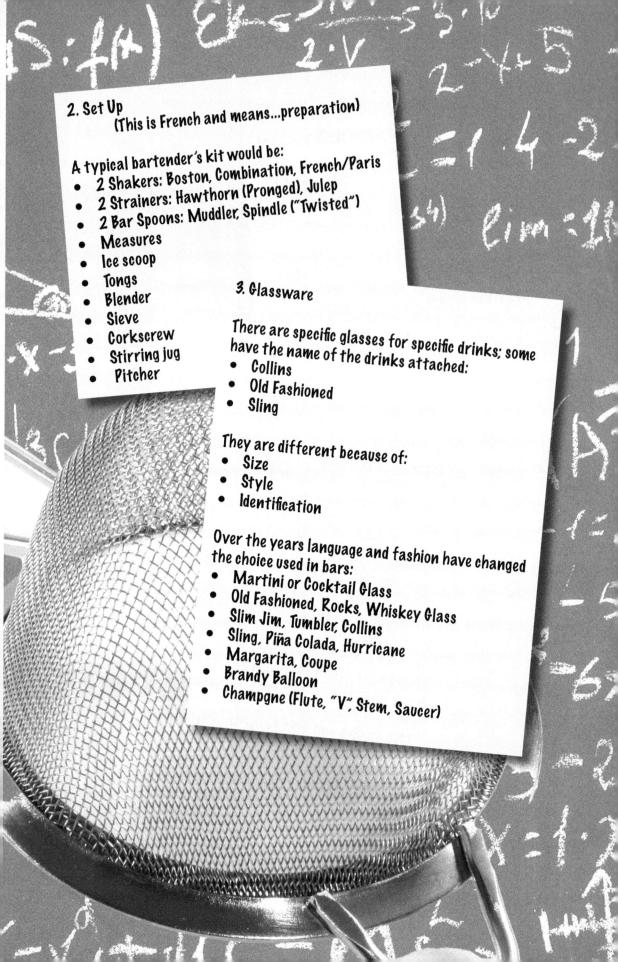

2. Set Up
(This is French and means...preparation)

A typical bartender's kit would be:
- 2 Shakers: Boston, Combination, French/Paris
- 2 Strainers: Hawthorn (Pronged), Julep
- 2 Bar Spoons: Muddler, Spindle ("Twisted")
- Measures
- Ice scoop
- Tongs
- Blender
- Sieve
- Corkscrew
- Stirring jug
- Pitcher

3. Glassware

There are specific glasses for specific drinks; some have the name of the drinks attached:
- Collins
- Old Fashioned
- Sling

They are different because of:
- Size
- Style
- Identification

Over the years language and fashion have changed the choice used in bars:
- Martini or Cocktail Glass
- Old Fashioned, Rocks, Whiskey Glass
- Slim Jim, Tumbler, Collins
- Sling, Piña Colada, Hurricane
- Margarita, Coupe
- Brandy Balloon
- Champgne (Flute, "V", Stem, Saucer)

Key Skills: Shaking
Stirring   Exposition
Blending   Demonstration
Building Drinks   Exercise
Layering "
Presentation

                    — Intermediate/Advance
Key Knowledge: Appreciation of qualities
            Taste
            e.g. Vodkas — contextual.

        /

        Basic understanding of attributes
        of ingredients:

        /   — how do they ~~attract~~ interact?

Predictable — getting a basic balance.

-Tuesday, 22 April 2003

We are going to teach you the basic skils you need to work behind a cocktail bar:

1. How to Shake

2. How to read a recipe

3. How to work behind a bar = your station

4. How to read an order—from the till printer and from a written docket

5. What is a cocktail?
• Original cocktail is a short drink in a cocktail glass
• Cocktail = all mixed drinks nowadays
• "Martini"–how the word has changed to be less precise. Cocktails are not a precise science.

6. The importance of the glass

7. How to stir—using a pitcher or shaker to stir

8. How to layer

9. How to flame

10. Clean up

4. Basic Equipment

Some equipment is good, some is badly made & difficult to use. You need to ensure the euipment behind your bar is good enough to allow you to do your job properly.

a) Shaker
- A shaker is used for getting drinks cold, as fast as possible.
- How you shake is important, it is a SKILL.
- Skills are developed through practice coupled with a will to succeed.

Boston
2 parts—one metal, one glass

Combination
Has its own strainer built in, splits into 3 parts

French/Paris
2 metal parts

b) Strainer
- 2-prong Hawthorn
- 4-prong Hawthorn
- Julep

c) Spoons
- Spindle ("Twisted")
- Muddler

d) Muddlers
- Rolling pin
- Muddler spoon

e) Stirring Jug/Martini Pitcher

f) Sieve

All this stuff was typed out as handouts for students to take home.

5. Juices

Cocktail bars tend to have 3 types of juices:
- Freshly squeezed
- Fresh from the supplier
- Carton juices

a) Freshly Squeezed
- Usually lime and lemon (sometimes orange) is squeezed on a juicer then strained and bottled.
- Lasts 2 to 3 days, and MUST be kept chilled at the correct temperature.
- NOTE: This can change according to the quality of the fruit bought.
- The result is usually EXCELLENT quality but it is EXPENSIVE.
- You need to ensure that you cost your drinks accordingly.

b) Fresh from the Supplier
- In London there are many fresh juice suppliers.
- They sell lemon, lime, orange, grapefruit (now even cranberry and tomato).
- The prducts are juiced in a factory daily and supplied to bars in the same manner as a dairy product.

NOTE: You should strain the lemon and lime juices.
Lasts 2 to 3 days (tomato juice lasts 1 day)
(Look out for inconsistent, pithy and old stock)

c) Carton
Tetrapak carton juices are the mainstay of bars and they are easy to find. They are a long way from fresh but some are better than others (especially tomato & orange)
- Orange
- Grapefruit
- Pineapple
- Tomato
- Lychee
- Cranberry
-

6. Pureés

Instead of fresh fruit, bartenders often use pureés, originally intended for kitchen/patisserie use.
- Some juice suppliers now make them.
- Pureés tend to be 10% sugar & fresh fruit and they often come frozen in 1L packs.
- They are often most cost—as well as time—efficient.

- White peach
- Raspberry
- Mango
- Passion fruit
- Strawberry
- Kiwi

Last a few days one opened/defrosted.
Frozen product has a lengthy shelf life—please check each individual pack for exact expiry dates.

7. Nectars

Some nectars are used in cocktails
- Peach
- mango
- Guava
- Passion fruit

These can be likened to 'watery' pureés and tend to be commercial products, often full of flavouring and stabilisers.
Shelf life is between 7 and 10 days once opened.
Please check each individual pack for exact expiry dates.

8. Syrups

In the (not too distant) past, bartenders had to use loaf sugar, ground or shaved down to which they would add warm water to produce a syrup for drinks. This can now be bought bottled and is called syrup de gomme, bar sugar or simple syrup.

You can make it (chefs do) but it is cheap to buy. The advantage of the bought product is primarily consistency and labour saving.

There are also flavoured syrups:

- Most common is grenadine (a red syrup originally made from pomegrantes) orgeat, and almond syrup
- Others include: passion fruit, mango, strawberry, raspberry

NOTE: There is a wide variety in quality

9. Cordials

The cordial is an old Victorian favourite. It is a way to preserved fruit drink products. The most common is Lime Cordial—Rose's remains popular amongst bartenders. It is the last survivor of the 1800s. Flavours include Blackcurrant.

10. Bitters

- Angostura: Angostura, Venezuela
- Peychaud: Herbesaint-based red bitters from New Orleans
- Orange: Hoppe, Holland
- Peach: Hoppe, Holland

NOTE: Campari is also a bitter.

11. Milk Products

- 1/2 and 1/2: Half milk, half cream mixed
- Milk: Use fresh not UHT, keep it chilled at the correct temperature
- Cream: Double or single is best, not whipping
- Eggs: Very few drinks use them, however egg white is used for binding citrus to spirit to produce froth. Fresh egg whites may make some people ill, so use packaged pasteurised egg whites for patisseries.

12. Spirits

- The base of a cocktail
- They can be split into dark spirits and white spirits
- The better the quality of the spirit the better the quality of the drink
- Specific gravities and weights are important when making certain drinks

a) Dark Spirits:
Rum: dark rum, double demerara, Jamaican, añejo
Whisky: scotch, malt, rye, bourbon, Irish
Brandy: Cognac, Armagnac

b) White Spirits:
Vodka: plain, flavoured, traditionally-flavoured
Gin: London, Plymouth, genever, sloe
Light rum: Cuban, Bacardi, agricole, cachaça
Tequila: silver, gold, añejo, reposado, mescal

13. Liqueurs

There are many, many types of liqueurs. They can be categorised in a variety of ways:

By Maker:
- Proprietary: Tia Maria, Cointreau and Baileys
- Generic: blue curaçao, crème de peche and kummel

OR

By Style of Flavour:
- Fruit: Cointreau, Fraise and Archers
- Coffee, Creams: Baileys, Kahlua and cacao & chocolate
- Herbs: Kummel, Chartreuse and Galliano

OR

By Base Spirit:
- Brandy based: Cointreau, Van der Hum
- Spirit based: Kummel, Jaegermeister
- Whisky based: Baileys, Drambuie, Southern Comfort
- Rum based: Tia Maria, Malibu, Koko Kanu

OR

By Method of Creation:
- Essence flavoured
- Juice flavoured
- Macerated

HOW I INVENT DRINKS

NEW PRODUCT: A NEW PRODUCT COMES ON THE MARKET
OR AVAILABLE   WE EXPERIMENT AND COME UP WITH A NEW DRINK
                LYCHEE + ROSE PETAL MARTINI
                CARAMEL MANHATTAN

NAME
OR CONCEPT   A BRAMBLE   MORE DRINK

                HONEY WALL

TWIST
ON A CLASSIC.

                ~~BEEF AFTER CLEOPATRA~~

                SUMMER BREEZE
                TREACLE

√
WK
GIN
DR
WS
BOUR
TEQ
LIQ
Brandy Sw Sour long shot strong cream

A template Dick used to develop a drinks menu.

173

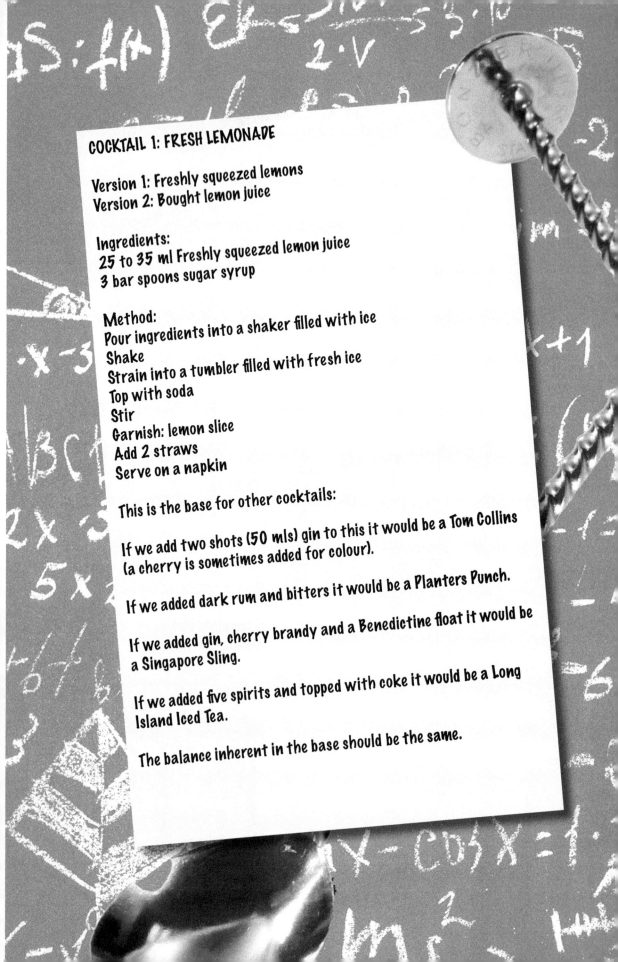

COCKTAIL 1: FRESH LEMONADE

Version 1: Freshly squeezed lemons
Version 2: Bought lemon juice

Ingredients:
25 to 35 ml Freshly squeezed lemon juice
3 bar spoons sugar syrup

Method:
Pour ingredients into a shaker filled with ice
Shake
Strain into a tumbler filled with fresh ice
Top with soda
Stir
Garnish: lemon slice
Add 2 straws
Serve on a napkin

This is the base for other cocktails:

If we add two shots (50 mls) gin to this it would be a Tom Collins
(a cherry is sometimes added for colour).

If we added dark rum and bitters it would be a Planters Punch.

If we added gin, cherry brandy and a Benedictine float it would be
a Singapore Sling.

If we added five spirits and topped with coke it would be a Long
Island Iced Tea.

The balance inherent in the base should be the same.

Bartender. -- Serve drinks.

Next Level — make drinks
— learnable skill.

Fresh Lemonade - Exercise

All fundamental skills.

Organisation
Hygiene — Directly affects taste.
Speed & Efficiency
LEMONADE
Visible
Equipment.
Ingredients
Presentation. Quality

Progression
Lemonade — Base
|
Tom Collins

Next Tequila Sunrise

| FRESH LEMONADE |

SHAKE

30 MLS   LEMON JUICE
15 MLS   SUGAR SYRUP

SHAKE WITH ICE
STRAIN OVER FRESH ICE

TOP WITH SODA
STIR
GARNISH: LEMON SLICE

TALL GLASS

| PLANTERS PUNCH | ORIGINAL RECIPE

SHAKE

50 MLS   MYERS RUM
30 MLS   LEMON JUICE
15 MLS   SUGAR SYRUP
DASH OF ANGOSTURA
SHAKE WITH ICE
STRAIN OVER FRESH ICE
TOP WITH SODA
STIR
GARNISH: ORANGE SLICE (+ CHERRY)

COCKTAIL 2: TOM COLLINS

The dirnk has its own history and its own style of glass. From this drink we are going to learn many lessons and how to make better cocktails.

Ingredients:
50 ml gin
25 ml lemon juice
3 tsp sugar

Method:
Shake
Pour into a glass
Top with soda
Garnish: cherry

An experienced bartender would recognise this drink as a famous classic.

COCKTAIL 3: TEQUILA SUNRISE

Ingredients:
50 ml Tequila
Orange juice
3 tsp Grenadine
Orange slice
Garnish: cherry

Method:
Fill a tall glass with ice
Pour in tequila
Top uop with orange juice
Add straws
Sink the grenadine to create a 'sunrise' effect
Garnish: orange slice & cherry

COCKTAIL 4: SEA BREEZE

The cocktail we now know as the Sea Breeze is a modern cocktail. One of the main reasons why is that cranberry juice has not been availiable for very long. This simple, easy, tall drink became omnipresent at parties and bars at the end of the last century and could easily de described as "the drink most served". To invent a drink as simple and popular as the Sea Breeze has been described as "the holy grail of bartending". Good, popular, simple drinks are rare.

Why was it so popular?

Customers like the taste, it was new, long and easy to drink, containing vodka with a clean flavour. There was no secret to it, no hidden "kick", no hidden ingredients.

Bartenders enjoyed its simplicity and speed of making. Most importantly, it uses just ingredients and ice, so apart from the alcohol, it is all neatly packed in cartons.

Ingredients:
50 ml vodka
Cranberry juice
Grapefruit juice
Garnish: lime wedge

'Build' Method:
Fill a tall glass with ice
Pour in vodka
Add juices in a ratio of 2 parts cranberry to 1 part grapefruit
Stir and garnish with lime wedge
Add 1 or 2 straws

more >>>>>>>>>>>>

COCKTAIL 4: SEA BREEZE—continued

'Shake Method:
Pour the vodka and juices into a shaker
Shake and pour into a tumbler full of ice
Add straws & agrnish as before

'Layering' Method:
Fill a tumbler with ice
Pour the grapefruit juice into the glass
Pour the vodka and cranberry juice into a shaker
Shake and pour over the grapefruit juice
The mix will float in 2 layers
Garnish: as before

Variations:
- Baybreeze: with pineapple juice
- Madras: with orange juice
- Summer Breeze: with (fresh, cloudy) apple juice & elderflower

COCKTAIL 5: COSMOPOLITAN

Ingredients:
35 ml lemon vodka
25 ml cranberry juice
20 ml Cointreau
Dash of lime juice, lime cordial & orange bitters
Garnish: Flamed orange slice (twist)

Method:
Pour all ingredients (except the orange slice) into a shaker full of ice
Shake & strain into a cocktail glass
Garnish with flamed orange slice

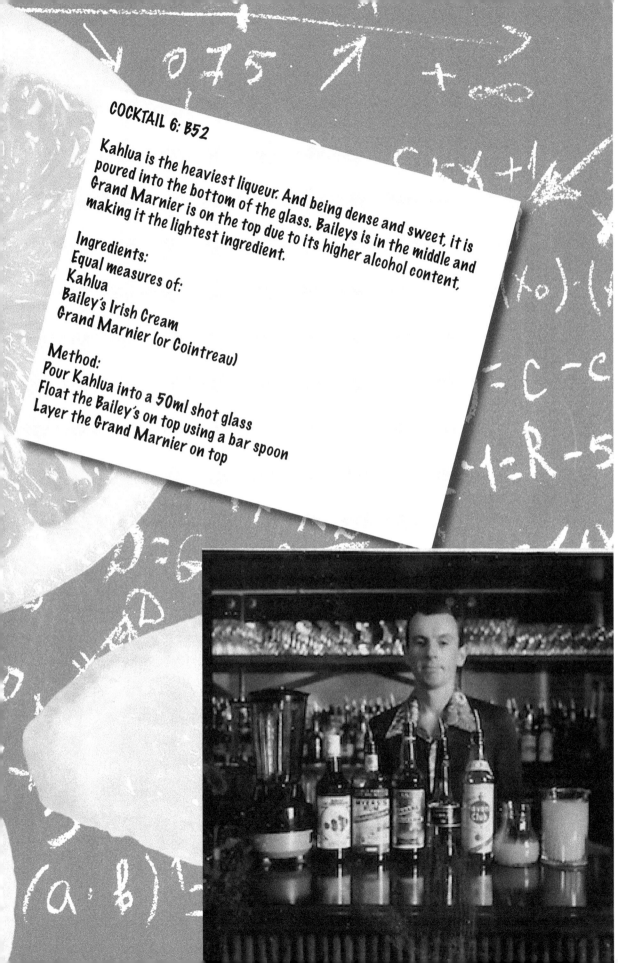

COCKTAIL 6: B52

Kahlua is the heaviest liqueur. And being dense and sweet, it is poured into the bottom of the glass. Baileys is in the middle and Grand Marnier is on the top due to its higher alcohol content, making it the lightest ingredient.

Ingredients:
Equal measures of:
Kahlua
Bailey's Irish Cream
Grand Marnier (or Cointreau)

Method:
Pour Kahlua into a 50ml shot glass
Float the Bailey's on top using a bar spoon
Layer the Grand Marnier on top

COCKTAIL 7: CLASSIC DRY GIN MARTINI

We have left the Classic Gin Martini until last because it seems to fill many bartenders with fear. Ironically, it is in fact the simplest—gin and vermouth stirred over ice and strained into a pre-chilled cocktail glass.

People who drink martinis often tell you which gin and vermouth to use (and how much). They are also likely to tell you how they want it served (so it couldn't be simpler!)

An example of a martini order:
Tanqueray Export Martini, straight up, very dry with 2 olives.

What they requested:
A particular brand of gin, stirred with very little vermouth, served with no ice and 2 olives on a cocktail stick placed in the drink.

If we do not receive these instrucitons we make the drink 'the house way' but you will generally need to know which garnish is preferred.

Ingredients:
75 ml gin
dash of dry vermouth
Garnish of choice

Method:
Pre-chilled cocktail glass
Add ice to a mixing jug and pour over the gin and vermouth
Stir and strain into the chilled glass
Garnish with an olive, lemon twist or cocktial onion

more >>>>>>>

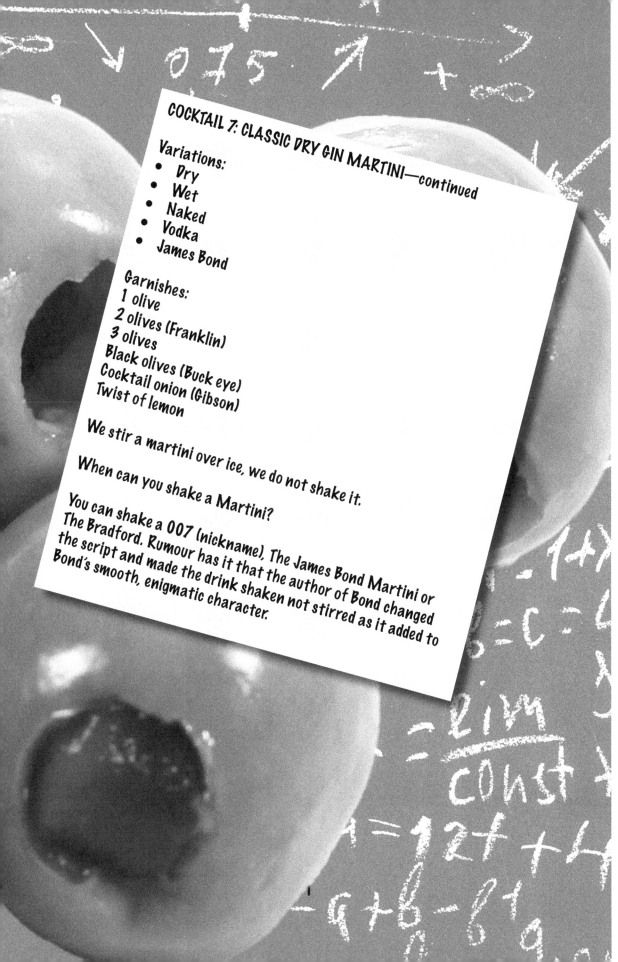

Variations:
- Dry
- Wet
- Naked
- Vodka
- James Bond

Garnishes:
1 olive
2 olives (Franklin)
3 olives
Black olives (Buck eye)
Cocktail onion (Gibson)
Twist of lemon

We stir a martini over ice, we do not shake it.

When can you shake a Martini?

You can shake a 007 (nickname), The James Bond Martini or The Bradford. Rumour has it that the author of Bond changed the script and made the drink shaken not stirred as it added to Bond's smooth, enigmatic character.

TWO TYPES Ⓐ PRECISION FOR FLAVOUR

AND Ⓑ YOUR BONUS! DAIQUIRI

MENTAL

TAKE TIME + TROUBLE — JUST BE CAREFUL NOT FLASHY (ALTHOUGH FLASHY IS ...

BUILD UP SPEED ...

MAKE IT RIGHT EVERYTIME FROM THE BEGINNING

THE BUILD UP SPEED -

REACHING ZEN BEHIND THE BAR

TURNING BORING REPETITION INTO JOY

PHYSICAL

BUT SPECIFICALLY NOTE YOUR MISTAKES/ERRORS

AND RECTIFY THEM!

IF YOU OVER POUR ON ALL KAMIKAZES

NOTE YOU DO

AND NEXT TIME DO NOT OVER POUR

ITS QUITE HARD BECAUSE IT IS RELEARNING

(OLD DOG NEW TRICKS — TEACHING AN OLD DOG THESAME TRICK

BUT A BIT DIFFERENT VERY HARD)

THE RELATIONSHIP BETWEEN DOING SOMETHING

AND THINKING ABOUT DOING IT AND CHANGING THAT

IS PHYSICAL !!)

ACCURACY IN CONTINUITY

TOEING THE LINE!!

THIS SHOULD BE SIMPLE

① THE RECIPE IS WRITTEN DOWN

② IT IS ACCURATE

③ YOU MAKE IT LIKE THAT

IT IS NOT A DICTATORSHIP
WE CAN TELL THIS BECAUSE IF THE DRINKS ARE
NOT THE SAME   MAYBE IT SHOULD BE?
DICTATORSHIP OF THE RECIPE.
DECIDE HOW TO MAKE THEM
THEN MAKE THEM LIKE THAT

THE ONLY OTHER REASON IS COMMUNICATION
THATS WHY YOU ARE ALL HERE

ORDER OF DRINK MAKING
BEERS + WATER + WINE INITIAL
LONG DRINKS FIRST
DRINKS ON ICE SECOND
SHORT DRINKS LAST
MARTINIS FINALLY.

ASK ME ABOUT CLASSIC COCKTAILS TILL YOU ARE BORED

CHAPTER FIVE

WHERE WAS DICK?: A RAMBLLING LIST

It's the only map Dick left of where he worked, so this is like a "Where's Wally" game: We know most the the places that were touched by Dick's guiding hand. Email at Dick's Page on the Mixellany website if you know of one we might have missed.
(That's "Where's Waldo" in the US.)

WHERE WAS DICK: PART 1

TRAINED IN CLUB MANAGEMENT AT THE NAVAL & MILITARY CLUB, PICCADILLY, IN 1977, UNDER HIS UNCLE PETER GURNEY

TRAINED AS A COCKTAIL BARTENDER AT THE ZANZIBAR CLUB [ALONG WITH FRED TAYLOR] UNDER ROY COOK

BARMANAGER AT SOHO BRASSERIE [WITH FRED TAYLOR]

Independent bars   vs   Hotel Bars
                                        + chains
           Naval + Military Club   (started handing hotel
                                       lounge bars onto indy operators)

        Trained at Zanzibar Club   — Roy started Groucho
                |
           Fred's Club
                | young persons membership Club
           Dick's Bar   (with Nick Strangeway)
Now Zedel — The Atlantic   for Oliver Peyton
                |

           Cafe de Paris   —   Jasper Eyears
                                     Cranbry Hill
        The Match Group ⟶ Tony Colgniano + Giovanni
        Lonsdale   with Henry Besant   Burdi
                          + Claire Smith   (Charles
Researching History   Verant
Internet + New books)   Taking Bar staff to Vineyards
We were looking for Access to good products
                    Havana Club Rum — Polish vodka
                                        Wyborowa
   Fresh juices — Quality

                                     TV chefs showing its a
                     Class Magazine   good career choice
    The Bar Show   _____ + Theme Magazine
                      Training days across the UK.
More respect   realising the best bars were not in London
                                        Leeds
Lots of Europeans workers   Manchester
  + Aussie + South Africans   Edinburgh
coming to London
with high standards
              traditionally
     Italian + French + Swiss   South Africans Aussies Poles
                                Swedes Slovakians

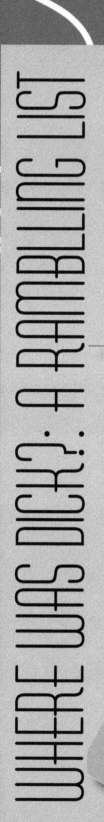

WHERE WAS DICK?: A RAMBLLING LIST

WHERE WAS DICK: PART 2

CLUB 97, HONG KONG

MOSCOW CLUB, SOHO, LONDON

SOHO BRASSERIE (AGAIN)

DOME, KING'S ROAD, CHELSEA, LONDON

GROUCHO CLUB, SOHO, LONDON (WITH FRED TAYLOR)

15 JAPAN MATCHES IMPERIAL MATCH

STREET LONDON W1V 5AP
TEL: 0171-439 4685
FAX: 0171-437 0373

THE GROUCHO CLUB

NINETEEN

G97

DICK BRADSELL
Head Barman
Club 97

NINETEEN 97
9 LAN KWAI FONG
CENTRAL HONG KONG
5-260303-4

Cocktails

Daquiri (Classic / Strawberry / Mango / Raspberry) £7.00
havana club 3yr, fresh lime juice, sugar syrup

Mojito £7.00
havana club 3yr, fresh lime juice, brown sugar, fresh mint, soda

Mai Tai £7.50
mount gay, bacardi, apricot brandy, orange curaçao,
fresh lime juice, fresh lemon juice, almond syrup, bitters

Caipirinha £7.00
cachaça, fresh lime juice, brown sugar

Mint Julep £6.50
buffalo trace bourbon, brown sugar, bitters, fresh mint

Manhattan £7.50
canadian club, martini dry / sweet, bitters

Rusty Nail £6.75
chivas regal, drambuie

Brandy Alexander £7.50
reserve de martell, dark crème de cacao, nutmeg, cream

Margarita £6.7!
sauza tequila, cointreau, fresh lime juice

Sours (Vodka / Gin / Whisky / Brandy / Amaretto) £6.
spirit, fresh lemon juice, sugar syrup

Dr Henderson £6
fernet branca, crème de menthe

a
the alfonso
brandy, sugar, bitters & champagne

amaretto sour
amaretto & lemon juice with bitters 4.00

americano
italian vermouth, campari & soda 4.50

b
b 52
kahlua, baileys & cointreau 4.00

bacardi cocktail
white rum, lime & grenadine 4.00

banana da...

blue n...
tequila, blue curaçao...

the bramble
gin, lemon juice & blackberry liqueur 4.50

brandy alexander
brandy, cacao & cream 4.50

brandy milk punch
brandy milk & sugar 4.00

brave bull
tequila & kahlua 4.00

bull...

coffee chaser
grand marnier, tia maria & cream + hot coffee 4.50

coffee flip
brandy, port, sugar, egg & cream 4.50

corpse reviver
brandy, calvados & italian vermouth 4.50

WHere Was Dick: Part 3

Manager at Fred's Club, London

FREDS ABC OF COCKTAILS & MIXED DRINKS

screaming orgasm
bailey's, tia maria, grand marnier & cream 5.50

screwdriver
double vodka & orange 4.50

sea breeze
vodka, cranberry & grapefruit 4.00

shirley temple
ginger ale & grenadine 2.50

sidecar
brandy, lemon, triple sec 4.50

sicilian kiss
southern comfort &amaretto 4.50

silver bullet
vodka & kummel 4.50

silver cloud
genever gin & kummel 4.50

silver streak
gin & kummel 4.50

singapore sling
gin, lemon, sugar with cherry brandy 4.50

sloe comfortable screw (up against the wall)
sloe gin, southern comfort & orange (with galliano) 4.50/5.00

snowball
advocaat & lemonade 3.50

sours
desired spirit, lemon & sugar with bitters 4.00

spider
brandy & green crème de menthe 4.00

stinger
brandy & white, crème de menthe 4.50

straits sling
gin, lemon, sugar, cherry brandy & benedictine 5.50

t

tequila sunrise
tequila, orange juice & grenadine 4.50

the thunderer
vodka, cassis & parfait amour 4.50

tigers milk
calvados, milk, sugar & spices 4.00

tom collins
gin, lemon, sugar & soda 4.00

v

vera litz
gin & cointreau 4.00

vodka collins
vodka, lemon, sugar & soda 4.00

vodka espresso
frozen vodka, espresso coffee, sugar 4.00

w

whisky mac
whisky and ginger wine 4.00

whisky sour
american whisky, lemon, sugar & soda 4.00

white lady
gin, lemon, triple sec & egg white 4.50

white russian
vodka, kahlua & cream 4.50

woo woo
vodka, cranberry, peach schnapps & lime 5.00

Fred would like to say that all cocktails ar[e] one-third off between 6 & 8 pm every da[y] Saturday when he says you can have th[…] likewise between 8 & 10 pm

design & cartooning: etienne

Fred's Club
Me + Fred Taylor owns Taqueria Daquin Naturel loved Daquiris so we set out to learn stuff

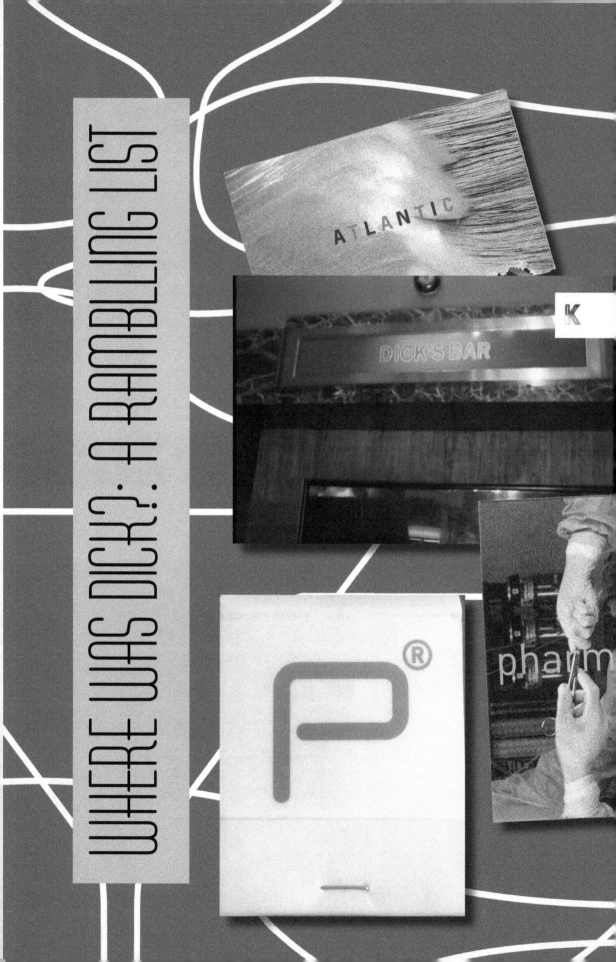

WHERE WAS DICK?: A RAMBLLING LIST

WHERE WAS DICK: PART 4

DETROIT BAR, COVENT GARDEN, LONDON

DICK'S BAR AT THE ATLANTIC BAR AND GRILL, PICCADILLY, LONDON

DETROIT BAR, COVENT GARDEN, LONDON

PHARMACY, NOTTING HILL, LONDON

matchec1
45-47 clerkenwell road london ec1m 5rs

dick bradsell

t:020 7250 4002
f:020 7250 4166

e:matchbar@aol.com
m:07990 978 166

the **playe**

8-12 Broadwick Street London W1V 1FH

Tel 0171 494 9125
Fax 0171 494 9126

matchbar
37-38 margaret street london w1n 7fa

dick bradsell

t:020 7499 3443
f:020 7499 3553

e:matchbar@aol.com
m:07990 978 166

WHERE WAS DICK: PART 5

DEVELOPED OPENING PROGRAMMES FOR:

MATCH BAR, CLERKENWELL, LONDON

MATCH BAR W1, LONDON

SOSHO MATCH, LONDON

REVOLUTION BARS, UK

ALFRED'S, LONDON

EGG, LONDON

at MatchEc1 when you rented/bought
a flat you got a ticket for a free
drink at your new local ... MatchEc1
Then you would be introduced to the manager
and he would buy you another drink.
Friends for life .....!

A "So" method that works...!

Sign people up to club as members
by this method

Get hold of their email or mobile
number and invite them to
meet door person at club
(early-ish or at there convenience)

for a day. Tell them it's to make
Show them round club + more of "a club"
Tell them the rules as required
bonuses by

To cure man

Then tell them ...   £4..0o

If you have a party on monday
we give you a free bottle of tequil
(and buy them a drink !!) [£10.oo for that
(monday) is members party night...
[we have a party for the members.]

oh + do Tequila Tuesday

WHERE WAS DICK: PART 6

DEVELOPED OPENING PROGRAMMES FOR:

TSUNAMI, LONDON

SUMOSAN, LONDON

RIVERWALK, LONDON

MONTES, LONDON

CAFÉ DE PARIS, LONDON

FLAMINGO, LONDON

HARLEM, LONDON

CONRAN@CHELSEA, LONDON

The Hakka (house c
Fill a large fancy glass with
pour in
25mls peach puree
50mls coconut water
25mls pineapple juice
add
25mls Tuaca liqueur
25mls ~~Creole Shrub~~ orar
then more crushed ice a
1 dash Angostura bitter
2 dashes orange bitters
3 dashes cardamon ess
garnish with lots of le
then douse with
25mls yellow chatreuse ano
25mls polish spirit and set it alight
add two straws

barsolutions
37-38 margaret street london w1n 7fa

dick bradsell

Falanana
Into a shaker full of rock ice pour:
25mls blue curacao
50mls freshly juiced pineapple
25mls cream
10mls Germana cachaca
shake vigorously
strain into frozen cocktail glass
garnish: pineapple spear & cherry

SHAKE

Chrysathemum Caiphirina
Chop a lime into small pieces
place in a glass shaker
cover with 3 teaspoons homemade chrysanthumum syrup
muddle
add
50mls Germana cachaca
a scoop of crushed ice
shake
pour into ~~old fashioned~~ wobbly rocks

MUDDLE

OWNING AND OPERATING THE CONSULTANCY BAR SOLUTIONS WHICH OPENED:

LONSDALE, LONDON (WITH HENRY BESANT)

TAQUIERIA (WITH FRED TAYLOR)

HAKASAN, SOHO, LONDON

23 ROMILLY STREET, SOHO, LONDON

DICK'S PAGE
COCKTAILS FROM THE BARTENDER DICK BRADSELL

Dick Bradsell is undoubtedly the finest bartender in the UK. He has been responsible for creating the majority of today's 'contemporary classics' and trained many of London's leading bartending lights. We are proud to say that Dick worked behind the bar here at Lonsdale between 2002 and 2004.

ROSE PETAL MARTINI - £8.00
Bombay Sapphire stirred with Lanique rose liqueur, lychee juice and Peychaud Bitters.

POLISH MARTINI - £8.00
Luksusowa Vodka stirred with Zubrowka Bison Grass Vodka, Krupnik Honey Liqueur and apple juice.
Created for his father in law, Viktor Sarge.

WIBBLE - £7.00
Plymouth Gin, sloe gin, fresh grapefruit juice, crème de mure, lemon juice and sugar.
Created in 1999 at the Player, London, England.

RUSSIAN SPRING PUNCH - £8.00
Stolichnaya Vodka stirred with lemon juice, sugar, topped with champagne and crowned with crème de cassis.
One of the best drinks to emerge in the 90s.

BRAMBLE - £7.00
Bombay Sapphire Gin stirred with lemon juice and sugar served over crushed ice and laced with crème de mure.
Created in the mid-80s at Fred's Club, Soho, London, England.

CAROL CHANNING - £8.00
Raspberry eau de vie and liqueur topped with champagne.
Created and named in 1984 after the famously large mouthed American comedienne Carol Channing because of appearance in the film 'Thoroughly Modern Milly'.

WHERE WAS DICK?: A RAMBLLING LIST

THE GREEN FINGERNAIL @ 23 ROMILLY STREET

Lola

Every Wednesday at The Green Fingernail
23 Romilly Street (Downstairs)
Soho London

www.clublola.co.uk

WHERE WAS DICK: PART 8

BARTENDING AT:

THE COLONY ROOM CLUB, SOHO, LONDON

PINK CHIHUAHUA, SOHO, LONDON

WHERE WAS DICK?: A RAMBLING LIST

EL CAMINO MEXICANO

Dick Bradsell

25-27
Brewer Street
London
W1F 0RR

Tel: 020 7734 7711
Mobile:

EL CAMION MEXICANO

the pink Chihuahua

Dick even had time to think about a cocktail book he wanted to write.

WHERE WAS DICK: PART 9

DICK'S LAST PLAN TO OPEN A BAR WAS NAMED THE LITTLE BLACK PUSSY-CAT WHICH WENT THROUGH TWO EN-VISIONMENTS. THE FIRST WAS WITH FRED TAYLOR AND THE LATE HENRY BESANT. THE LAST WAS WITH ELINE SOO YUN BROSMAN, JARED BROWN, AND ANISTATIA MILLER

Transcribed from voice recording taken by Eline on 31/07/2015

-Right. This Player. I'm thinking, if it's been totally redone, the whole place that's a eh…got to rebuild that place. And come down that stairway into a big room. We have got our friend from Leeds (Mal Evans) who wants to do it and running all their ideas. We've also got Anistatia and Jared, and they have their ideas and maybe the five of us, that's five? Get together and talk about it. Now, I didn't talk to Simon about this project but he talked to me about projects. What he's saying we should do is, I should do, is a Dick's bar, because Dick's Bar is what this city needs. I want to enter into that idea and discuss. There will be lots of interest in that kind of thing. But well.. (pause) we'll have to talk about it. Doing something grand is a good idea. I can't work too hard because of my health but I reckon we can do something absolutely fantastic! But we've got to talk to our friends and these are all the best people… I don't want to do some ponce place.. I'm thinking as that's the original place where "Dick's Bar", the TV series was done –which was pretty crap- but it was done there. And Anistatia and Jared on board, we should do a TV series, a cocktail series. I don't know what we should call it. I need to sort that out first because it will be a problem point between everyone. How about: "The BARTENDERS" right? Like that. Or "The PROFES-SIONALS"! …And we give people all the recipes to all the cocktails all the years, but the right ones. I can see that a lot of argument… etc. etc.. But it could really help the project financially.

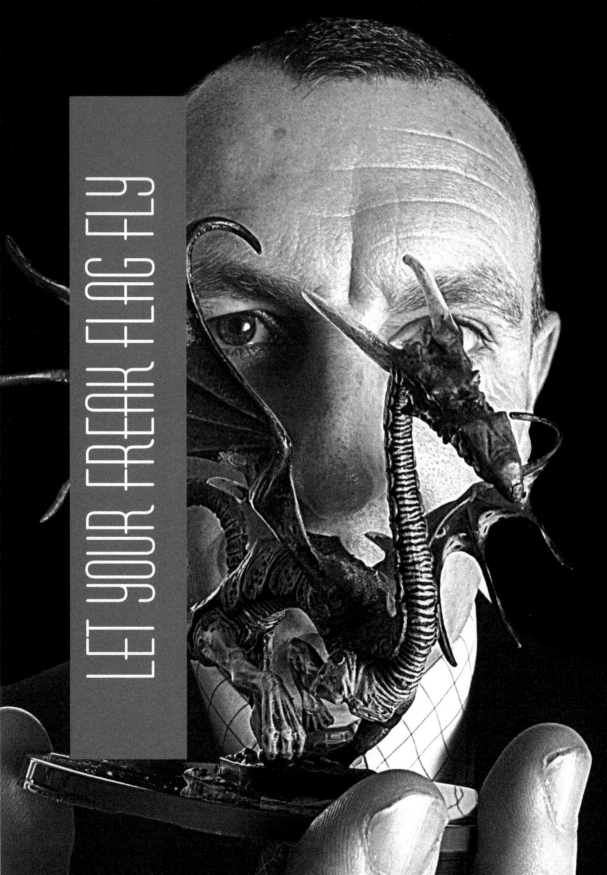

LET YOUR FREAK FLAG FLY

HARRIET STONE SISTER
DWARVEN HEALER (MIDWIFE)

HARRIET STONE FIST

was born into a rich and connected Dwarven dynasty: her future decided, her duty clear. At the age of 20 she disappeared.

An earthquake revealed a path to the surface and Harriet stumbled, blindly into the surface world. Lost, she hid under a tree and was found by some half elven forest renegades. A gang of city-born teenagers, who had fled to the forest and joined with a forest cult who worshipped the Fey. Harriet grew up learning their ways and showed an unusual ability of being able to disguise herself and deceive her friends. She was also cursed with "the Touch Of The Broom": Harriet was a witch!

She worshipped to the Fey and built her skills at spell¬craft and deception, always using her powers for good. She became their healer and midwife. She was much loved despite her otherness. But her curse took its toll. She saw the dark things in life. The nasty side of families.

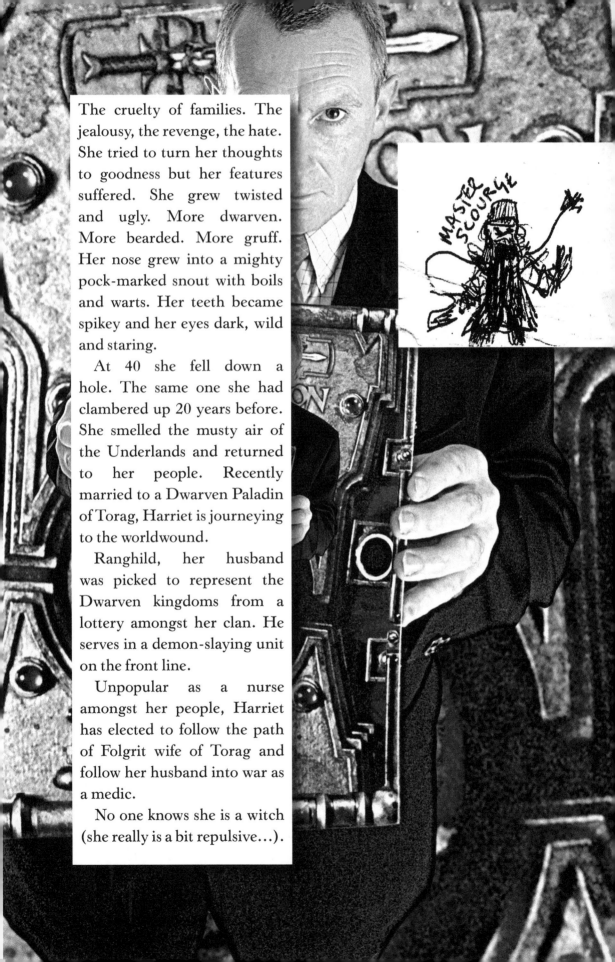

The cruelty of families. The jealousy, the revenge, the hate. She tried to turn her thoughts to goodness but her features suffered. She grew twisted and ugly. More dwarven. More bearded. More gruff. Her nose grew into a mighty pock-marked snout with boils and warts. Her teeth became spikey and her eyes dark, wild and staring.

At 40 she fell down a hole. The same one she had clambered up 20 years before. She smelled the musty air of the Underlands and returned to her people. Recently married to a Dwarven Paladin of Torag, Harriet is journeying to the worldwound.

Ranghild, her husband was picked to represent the Dwarven kingdoms from a lottery amongst her clan. He serves in a demon-slaying unit on the front line.

Unpopular as a nurse amongst her people, Harriet has elected to follow the path of Folgrit wife of Torag and follow her husband into war as a medic.

No one knows she is a witch (she really is a bit repulsive…).

MASTER SCOURGE

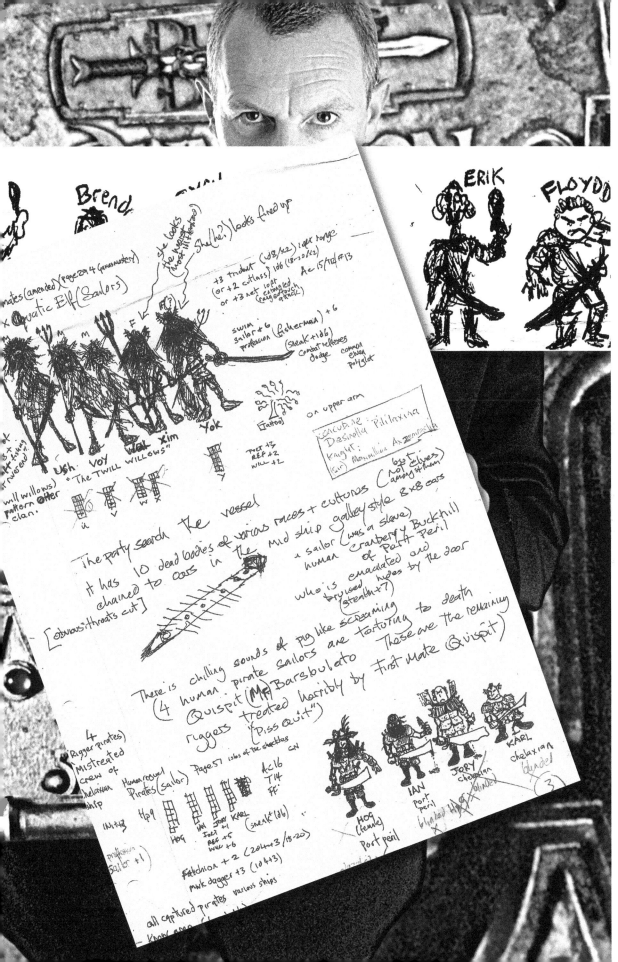

Brend...

ERIK **FLOYD**

she looks fired up
she looks the worst (most withered)

mates (amended) page 294 (gamemastery)
Aquatic Elf (Sailors)

+3 trident (d8/x2) 10ft range
(or +2 cutlass) 106 (18-20/x2)
or +3 net 10ft (entangled) (range/touch attack)
Ac 15/17/#13

swim
sailor +6
profession (fisherman) +6
(Sneak +106)
Combat reflexes
dodge common
elven
polyglot

[tattoo]
on upper arm

Concubine: Desinella Pililaxina
Knight:
(sir) Maximillian Axzenroslich

Fort +3
Ref +2
Will +2

Ush VOY WAL XIM YOK
"The TWILL WILLOWS"
twill willows)
pattern other clan.

The party search the vessel
It has 10 dead bodies of various races + cultures (not elves) (among them
chained to oars in the mid ship galley style 8x8 oars
[obvious throats cut]
a sailor (was a slave)
human cranberry Buckhill of Port Peril
who is emaciated and bruised hides by the door
(stealth +7)

There is chilling sounds of pig like screaming
(4 human pirate sailors are torturing to death
Quispit (Mr) Barsbulato These are the remaining
riggers treated horribly by First Mate (Quispit) "Piss Quit")

4 Rigger pirates)
Mistreated crew of chelaxian ship
[init +3]
profession sailor +1)

Human/elf Pirates (Sailor) Page 57 isles of the shackles CN
Hog9

Page 57 isles of the shackles Ac16 T14 FF

IAN JORY KARL
Fort +1
Ref +5 (sneak +1d6)
Will +6

Falchion +2 (20/14+3/15-20)
Mwk dagger +3 (10/+3)

all captured pirates various ships

HOG
IAN Port peril
JORY chelaxian
KARL chelaxian blinded
HOG (female) Port peril

The Sihedron Runes have an unknown power: Do they allow some form of contact or effect with the Runecolds?

You din't know that He could see
His Eye's upon you eternally?
Where the Seven goes He'll always know
A Oneway Telltale Controller Show

Where is the Runewell of Karzoug?

You seek him here, you seek it there
For you we sought him everywhere
It isn't here, he isn't here
So it isn't anywhere

Through which plane can we approach Xin Shalast?

Heard a tale long time ago
Of amazing city high in snow
Built tall and proud on a mountain head
But it isn't there. It is a dream that is dead

What sort of creatures exist in Xin Shalast?

Ancient Tails on ancient Beasts
Massive Building Black Rune Clad Meats
What is now is just a myth
The City is gone, it don't exist

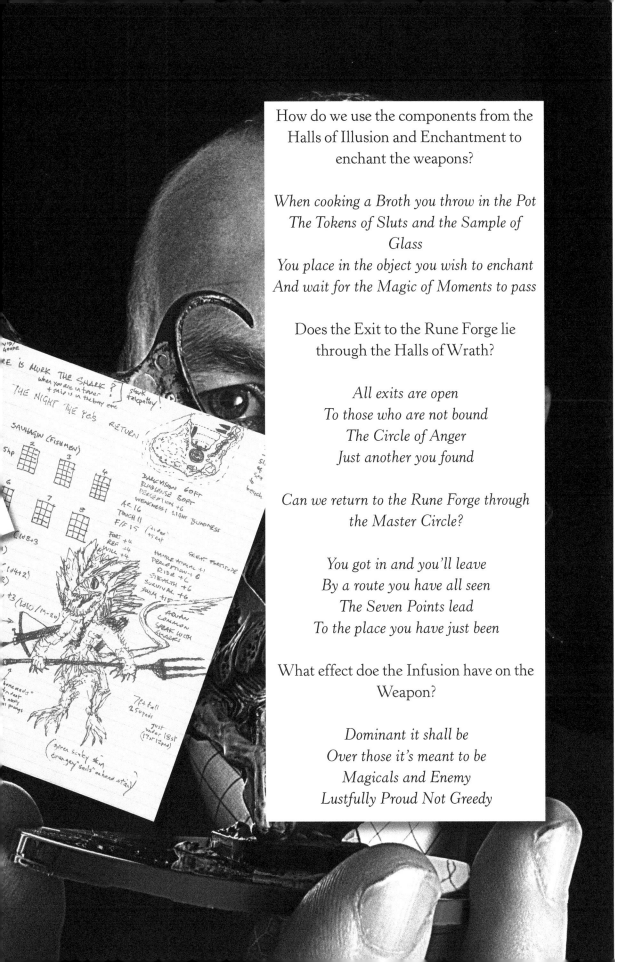

How do we use the components from the Halls of Illusion and Enchantment to enchant the weapons?

When cooking a Broth you throw in the Pot
The Tokens of Sluts and the Sample of Glass
You place in the object you wish to enchant
And wait for the Magic of Moments to pass

Does the Exit to the Rune Forge lie through the Halls of Wrath?

All exits are open
To those who are not bound
The Circle of Anger
Just another you found

Can we return to the Rune Forge through the Master Circle?

You got in and you'll leave
By a route you have all seen
The Seven Points lead
To the place you have just been

What effect doe the Infusion have on the Weapon?

Dominant it shall be
Over those it's meant to be
Magicals and Enemy
Lustfully Proud Not Greedy

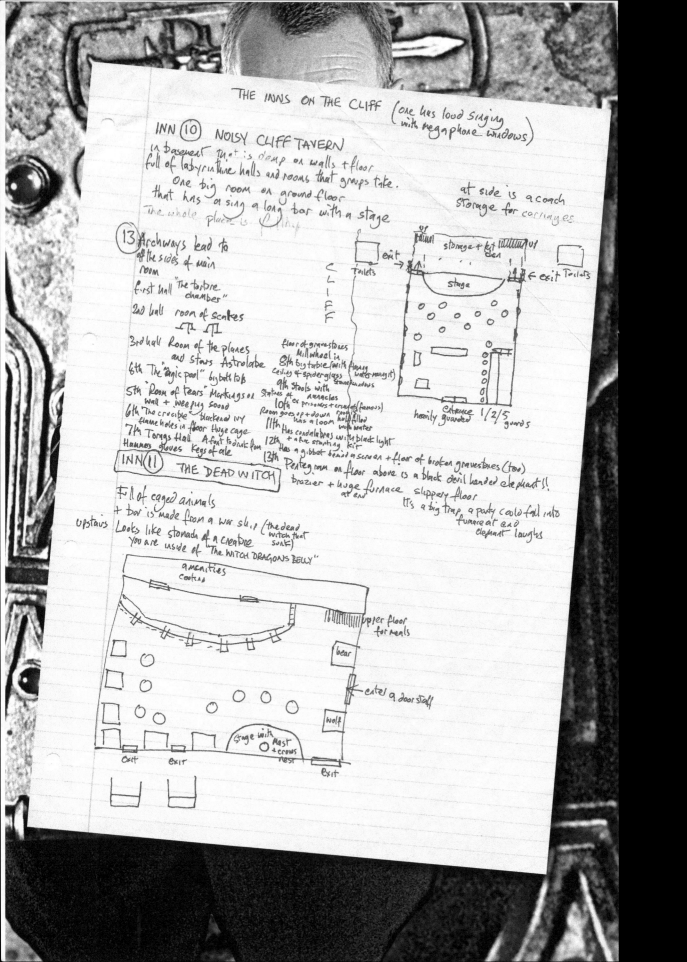

THE INNS ON THE CLIFF (one has loud singing with megaphone windows)

INN ⑩ NOISY CLIFF TAVERN

in basement that is damp on walls + floor
full of labyrinthine halls and rooms that groups take.
One big room on ground floor
that has a sing a long bar with a stage
The whole place is filthy

⑬ Archways lead to
off the sides of main
room

First hall "The torture chamber"

2nd hall room of snakes

3rd hall Room of the planes
and stars Astrolabe

4th The "magic pool" big bath tub

5th "Room of tears" Markings on
wall + weeping sound

6th "The crucible" blackened ivy
flame holes in floor Huge cage

7th Torags Hall A font to drink from
Hammers gloves Kegs of ale

floor of gravestones
Millwheel in
8th big table (with Hanging
Ceiling of spiderglass water-many it)
Stone windows
9th stools with
Statues of manacles
ex prisoners + criminals (famous)
10th
Room goes up + down room
has a loom hall filled
11th Has candelabras with black light
+ a fire standing kit
12th Has a gibbet behind a screen + floor of broken gravestones (too)
13th Pentegram on floor above is a black devil handed elephant!!
brazier + huge furnace slippery floor
at end
It's a big trap, a party could fall into
furnace at end
elephant laughs

at side is a coach
storage for carriages

up
storage + toilet
then

exit →

C L I F F

Toilets

stage

exit Toilets

heavily guarded

entrance 1/2/5
guards

INN ⑪ THE DEAD WITCH

Full of caged animals
+ bar is made from a war ship (the dead
witch that
Looks like stomach of a creature sunk)
you are inside of "The WITCH DRAGONS BELLY"

upstairs

amenities
cooking

upper floor
for meals

bear

enter a door staff

wolf

Stage with Mast
+ crows
rest

exit   exit   exit

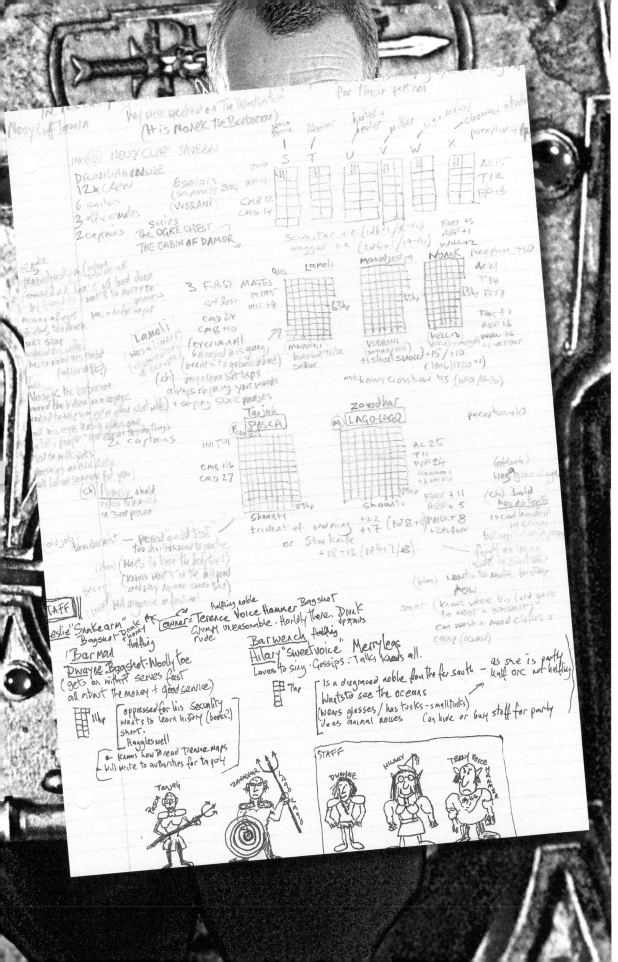

Noisy Cliff Tavern

They were wrecked on The Dead Witch   for their patron
(It is Norek the Barbarian)

INN (10) NOISY CLIFF TAVERN

DRINKING/INSIDE
12x CREW   Escalios
6 Sailors   (shipmate 204)
3 officer mates   (VUDRANI)
2 captains   SHIPS
          THE OGRE CHEST →
          THE CABIN OF DAMOR

S   T   U   V   W   X
                        AC 15
                        T 12
                        F/F 13

Scimitar +2 (1d6+1/18-20)
dagger +2 (1d4+1/+1-20)   Feet +5
                            REF +1
                            WILL +2

3 FIRST MATES   Lamoli   Manodjestya   Norek   perception +10
SM 30 FT   9HD   +1d4 TRS   AC 21
                   WILL +4   T 14
CMD 24   13h F/F 17
CMB +10
(Everciminali   MWANNI   VUDRANI   KELLID   Feet +7
  betrayed his gang) boatswain surname   Viking   REF 16
(wants to go back home) sailor   sword +5   winged WILL +6
                                  +1 short sword   +1 versus
(ch) very clean but lisps   +5/+10
  always rhyming your words   1 heavy crossbow +3 (1d10/19-20)
  + saying stock phrases

Norek the barbarian   Tanjah   Zovadhar
shared the kitten...   PASCA   LAGO-LAGO   perception +10
                   INIT +1
2x captains   CMB +16   AC 25
                   CMD 27   T 11
                                        F/F 24
(ch) lovely +bald
  refers to himself   (old ish)
  in 3rd person   Shoanti   (ch) bald
                   trident of warning +22   has no teeth
                      +17 (1d8+11)
  or Starknife
  +18 +13 (1d4+7/×3)

STAFF
Leslie "Snakearm"   Owner = Terence Voice Hammer Bagshot
  Bagshot - Drunk   Halfling noble   Drunk
  + horny Halfling   Grumpy unreasonable. Hardly there. Drunk
1 Barman   rude
Dwayne Bagshot-Woolytoe   Barwench   Halfling
(gets on with... serves fast Hilary "Sweetvoice" Merrylegs
all about the money + good service) Loves to sing. Gossips. Talks knows all.

  oppressed for his sexuality   Is a disgraced noble from the far south — as she is partly
  wants to learn history (books?)   Wants to see the oceans   half orc not halfling
  short.   (Wears glasses / has tusks - small tusks)
  Haggles well   Does animal noises   Can hide or buy stuff for party
  • knows how to read treasure maps
  - will write to authorities for the pay

STAFF
DWAYNE   HILARY   TERRY VOICE HAMMER

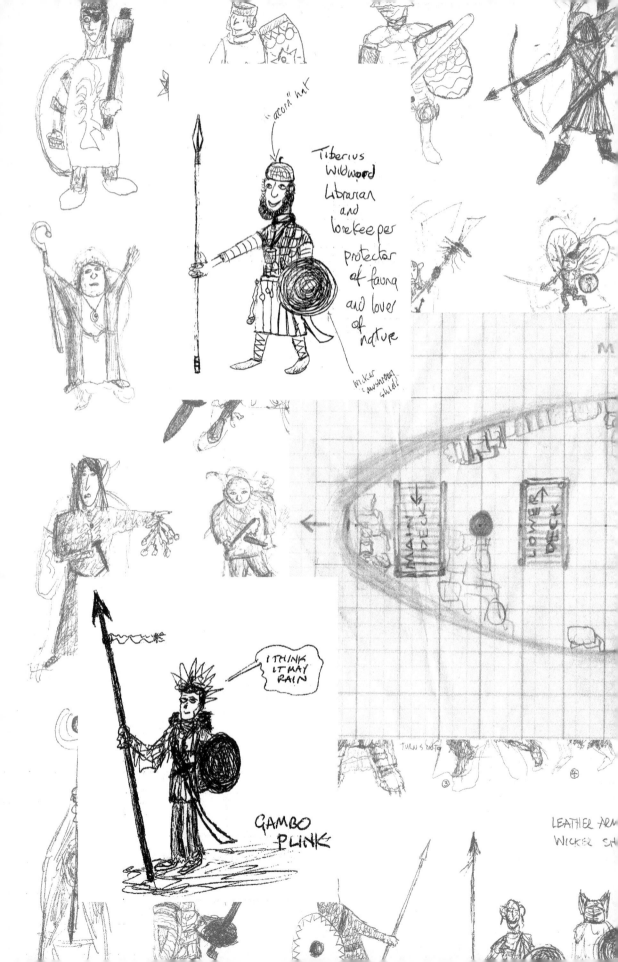

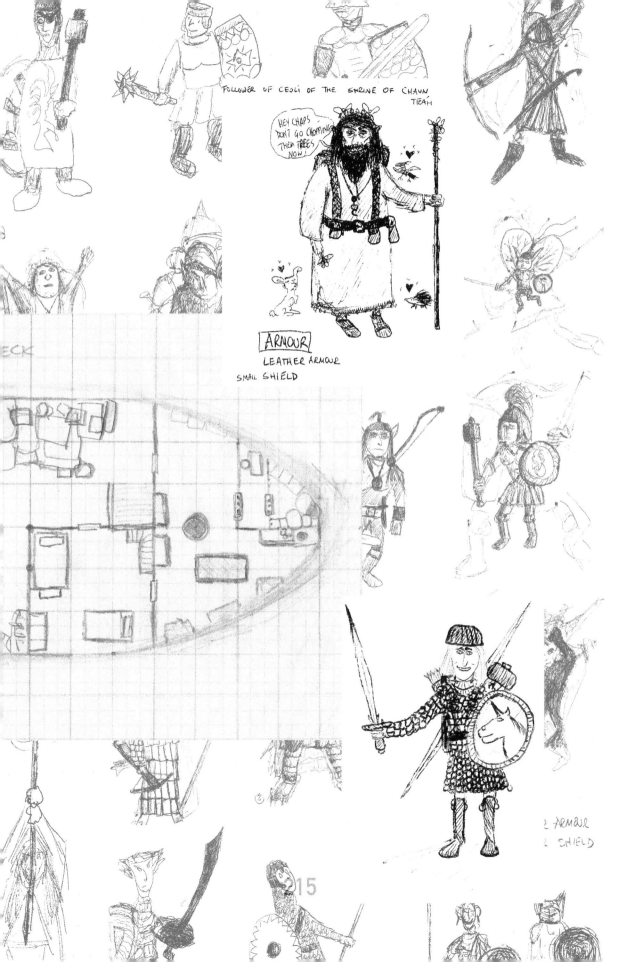

FOLLOWER OF CEOLI OF THE SHRINE OF CHAUN TEAH

HEY CHAPS DON'T GO CHOPPING THEM TREES NOW!

ARMOUR
LEATHER ARMOUR
SMALL SHIELD

R ARMOUR
L SHIELD

In Kimbi-Land

All my bread is moist
  My milk has yet to turn
  The sun shines in my night time
  And I'll not want to yearn

But way down in Kimbi-land
They just laugh at me.
They do not see
      the things I see.

They haven't been
      where I have been.

They do not know
      the things I know,

They do not go
      where I do go.

So cosseted it is
This hollow walk
      to the end of days.

Yet when they sleep
      they dream my dream.

(All my bread is moist
My milk is yet to turn
The sun shines in my night time
And I'll not want to yearn)

DICK ©2014

And he wrote poetry
when the mood struck.
Same with drawing—
Dick drew and wrote
and drew and...

In my life
The happiest I have been
Is in your arms

Is in your arms
The happiest I have been
  In my life

The happiest I have been
In my life
Is in your arms

In my life
Is in your arms
The happiest I've been

In the midst of date
When I am beset
I am reminded
by a colour &
like your eyes
A shade of olive
That could be your skin
Or something that
I want to share with yo
And I think of you

It is water to my thirst
the sleep at end of day

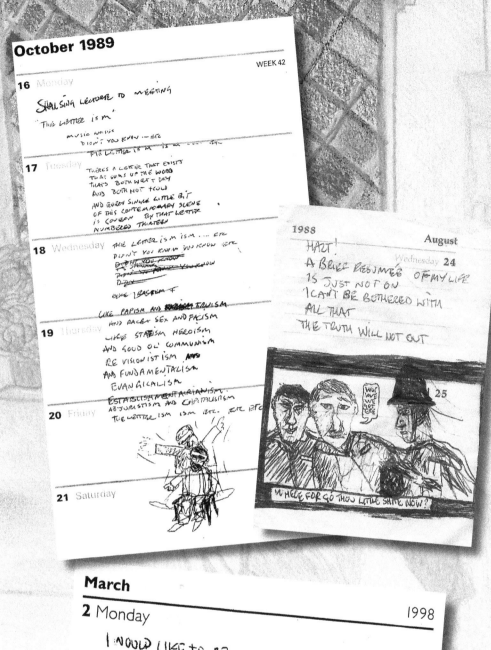

October 1989

WEEK 42

16 Monday

SHALL SING LECTURE TO MEETING
"THIS LETTER IS M"
MUSIC NOISE
DIDN'T YOU KNOW — ETC
THE LETTER IS M IS M ... ETC

17 Tuesday

THERE'S A LETTER THAT EXISTS
THAT SUMS UP THE WORLD
THAT'S BOTH WET + DRY
AND BOTH HOT + COLD
AND EVERY SINGLE LITTLE BIT
OF THIS CONTEMPORARY SCENE
IS COVERED BY THAT LETTER
NUMBERED THIRTEEN

18 Wednesday

THE LETTER IS M IS M ... ETC
DIDN'T YOU KNOW YOU KNOW ETC
DIDN'T YOU KNOW
YOU KNOW
OUR LEADER +

19 Thursday

LIKE PAPISM AND TRUISM
AND RACE SEX AND FACISM
LIKE STATISM HEROISM
AND GOOD OL' COMMUNISM
REVISIONISTISM AND
AND FUNDAMENTALISM
EVANGELICALISM
ESTABLISHAMENTARIANISM
ABJURISTISM AND CAPITALISM
THE LETTER ISM ISM ETC ETC ETC

20 Friday

21 Saturday

1988   August

Wednesday 24

HART!
A BRIEF RESUMÉ OF MY LIFE
IS JUST NOT ON
I CAN'T BE BOTHERED WITH
ALL THAT
THE TRUTH WILL NOT OUT

25

WOT LOVE WE ...

WHERE FOR GO THOU LITTLE SHITE NOW?

March   1998

2 Monday

I WOULD LIKE TO BE
AN INVISIBLE PERSON
WHO MADE YOU HAPPY

3 Tuesday

WENT AROUND OPENING DOORS FOR YOU
STOPPING THE TRAFFIC AT THE
PELICAN CROSSING
BEFORE YOU GOT TO IT

4 Wednesday

BUT, I GUESS, AFTER A WHILE
IT WOULD BE FUCKING ANNOYING.

DICK'S music playlist

It's rough to simply read playlists. So we've built Dick's playlists on iTunes and Youtube Music. Use the QR codes or go to Dick's page @ Mixellany.com: http://www.mixellany.com/dick-s-page.html

CHAPTER SEVEN

① ROCK ON, DAVID ESSEX
HEARD THIS AT A FUNFAIR ON HOLIDAY WITH MY PARENTS IN THE
EARLY 70's. STILL SOUNDS AMAZING. BEST THING HE DID.

② DAVID BOWIE, 5 YEARS
I ADORED BOWIE AS A YOUTH. I WAS LISTENING TO THIS
WASHING UP IN KITCHENS ON SOUTH COAST HOTELS IN THE HOLIDAYS

③ JAMES BROWN GET UP OFFA THAT THING
I WAS A WANNABE SOUL BOY AND WE WOULD ALWAYS DANCE
TO THIS. IT GOT EVERYONE ON THE DANCE FLOOR.
I JUST WANTED TO DANCE, DANCE, DANCE WHEN I WAS YOUNG
IN ISLE OF WIGHT NIGHTCLUBS. THIS FILLED THE DANCE FLOOR

④ NEW ROSE IN TOWN, THE DAMNED
THEN THERE WAS PUNK. THE DAMNED WERE STUNNING AND VERY SILLY
SAW THEM IN PORTSMOUTH (LOST A TOOTH) AND SOUTHAMPTON (GOT BEATEN UP)
FABULOUS TIMES!

⑤ ROXY MUSIC VIRGINIA PLAIN
I WAS ANOTHER TEENAGE BOY IN HIS BEDROOM LISTENING TO MUSIC
DREAMING OF LONDON, THE BIG CITY, GLAMOUR AND HAVING FUN.
THEN ALONG CAME ROXY MUSIC.

⑥ B52's PLANET CLAIRE THE SCALA CINEMA, SQUATTING IN HACKNEY
IN LONDON LONDON WAS SO EXCITING. I GOT TO SEE THE B52's
EARLY B52's CONCERT FIRST CONCERTS. I STOOD THERE GRINNING WITH MY MOUTH OPEN. TRENDY
IS COOL. THEY ARE BRILLIANT.

⑦ BOTH SIDES NOW
WHEN FORD AND ADAM KIDRON OPENED FRED'S CLUB
ADAM BOUGHT A KARAOKE MACHINE AND I LEARNT TO SING MONDAYS WAS
THIS (SITTING ON A STOOL IN THE EMPTY DISCO BASEMENT) SILLY DICKS NIGHT

⑧ THESE ARE THE THINGS (THAT DREAMS ARE MADE OF) THE HUMAN LEAGUE
I SAW AN EARLY GIG AT THE VENUE IN VICTORIA. THEY WERE
FANTASTIC WITH FILM SCREENS AND A FAT BLOKE WITH A BEARD
SINGING.

My music
book
from BBC
6 music

(My baby does) Sculptures
good ~~for you~~ by the Rezillos

I am a changing man
Paul Weller

Calling Rastafari
by Culture

(Tony Hancock
The Artist)

music from The
Cameroon

Nigerian high like
Prince Nico

{ Emi dropped
them (+ the pistols)

↓ Sold 13 million
copies.

for a Nigerian record label
pay back for the pistols to
Sweet Mother
(Sweet Mother)

6 music

make
~~her~~ happy"

the fire

~~Wil~~ Smith

the lyrics!

Cherry dip
by Cloud
(a friend is a friend
by feelings)
↑
a bit punky
Canadian

Almost was good {
enough by Ohio
album ↑
magnolia wow!

from

~~love~~ is to Die
by Warpant well!

no its not
is to live
that's the lyric
is to not
Too

he
uneasy"
was it
there?

Why does 6 music
play my favourite
music all day long
Float on by the
Floaters

A boy at school
Hot chip

Get up offa that
thing! James Brown

about Jona Lewie's
school song

new song
he didn't hear it

cos its good

You made me
Suffer by
Andrew Brown
(I thought it
was you made
me supper!)

Marketed &
~~...~~ted b

...ving of this record prohi...

ON LOCATION

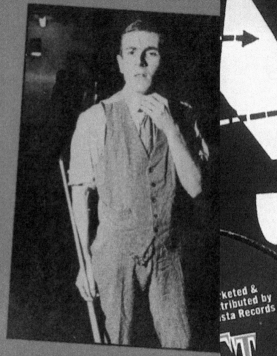

WHY ARE we printing a picture of Dave Wakeling playing pool? Well, it's like this. The Beat are all keen fans of *Photo Love Weekly*, the well known cult story romance magazine. (No kidding — that's where they got the title for "Hands Off, She's Mine!")

Anyway it seems Dave Steele has long nurtured a secret ambition to appear in one of these dramatic photo features and now he's managed just that, with Mr. Wakeling also appearing in a cameo role.

Our spies on the scene smuggled us out some outtake pictures (people smiling when they're supposed to be in high drama etc.) and we've put them together with a touch of affectionate humour to make a *very* different story which you can find on pages 34 and 35. The genuine article, however, appears in the issue of *Photo Love* which comes out on February 7.

Dave Wakeling — pictured on the set where the story was photographed — apparently enjoyed his taste of acting so much that he's signed up to star in another photo-novel later on. (Next week Ranking Roger in Play School?)

The other pool player pictured is none other than Dick Bradsell — co-writer of "Twist And Crawl" — who went along to lend moral support (and the bus fare home.)

eketed &
tributed by
rista Records

FEET 1
FEET 1 B 45
A

TWIST AND CRAWL
(The Beat/Bradsell)
Copyright Control
THE BEAT
Produced by Bob Sargeant

This is verifies of Dick's writing credit for the song "Twist and Crawl" (SMASH HITS, 22 Jan 1981, p. 12) along with the original record label.

GO·FE
RE

ENTRANCE

While My Guitar Gently Weeps by George Harrison

INTRODUCTION

by Jane Morgan

TRIBUTES

by Spike Merchant and John Melon

A MOMENT OF MUSICAL CONTEMPLATION

to Almost Cut My Hair by Cosby, Stills, Nash & Young

POEM

Eingang (Initiation) by Rainer Maria Rilke

...and the last playlist Dick created...

CLOSING WORDS

by Jane Morgan

FINAL SONGS

Twist & Crawl – The Beat & Dick Bradsell

Gangsters – The Specials

A Message To You Rudy – The Specials

Get Dancin' – Disco Tex and the Sex-o-Lettes

What is there left
to say about a life that was
lived to its fullest?

We'll let Dick have the last
word.

WHAT MAKES A MAN stylish? Clothes, attitude, something else? Maybe what makes a man stylish is wanting to be? Putting in the effort. Grooming, manners. Picking the right clothes. Maybe in the UK it is easier. There are many templates to follow. It is discussed and debated. There are so many great British and European designers and tailors.

As an older man I must not try to look too young or in-fashion. Nowadays there is a sort of bartender 'uniform' waistcoat beard tattoos arm cuff braces. I avoid that.

Maybe I'm not the right person to ask. I buy all my clothes from second hand stores.

I was super trendy as a youth. Now it is "mod" style. Like when I came to London. Short hair, tightish jeans, suit jacket. The eternal UK working class look. Mod/Skin/Casual. Or a good well-fitting suit and a good pair of shoes. Germans have my bar hero Charles Schumann. We have David Bowie, Bryan Ferry, etc. My style icon is my daughter's godfather Hamish Bowles. And Stephen Jones the milliner.

I am not so stylish nowadays. I avoid fashion for warmth and comfort.

Good health became more important.

The two best moments in my style life:

ONE: First day in London. An older lady from the 1960s ran down the escalator on the tube to hug me. *"Love your mod look love."* I had a dark blue, high-buttoned mohair suit, Cuban-heeled pointy-toed shoes. Yellow with blue check button down collar "Mick Jagger" double two shirt.

TWO: First day in New York on a trip to meet Dale DeGroff at the Rainbow Room. A couple stopped me and said, *"Love that suit guy!"* Gold two-tone two-piece with a red fleck and gold and red lining. Shining in the sunset.

Look good, feel good, love life. And it's free, just takes some effort. Makes life worth living.

When I next walk into a charity shop and find some bargain from the past that actually fits me well. Then I'm happy. Makes life worth living.

Pride in the appearance. The fantasy of cool. London rude boy.

Well turned out charmer. Or city gent.

"Best dressed chicken in town" playing as soundtrack in the background. Thanks.

I'm off to get that "new to me" suit.

MORE
RECIPES

MORE
STORIES

"Whenever you find Dick at a
bar, that's the place to be."

THE LAST BOTTLE DICK HANDED US...We nicknamed it FOG (short for Fear of God, having sniffed the liquid).

FRONT LABEL:
HAILI FOLGRIT HOW'S THEM [APPLES] DWARF GODDESS OF MID WIVES FOLGRIT... SEX+DRUGS AND ROCK

BACK LABEL:
Folgrit takes its name from the dwarf goddess of fucking. The blending of _____ from our torture gulags is an art handed down through generals. This marriage of ___ and ____ is matured in small blood-soaked barrels to produce an awful hideous warning disustif with a lingering aftertaste

MORE DICK

COMING SOON!